XML Parsing with PHP

by
John M. Stokes

 a php[**architect**] guide

XML Parsing with PHP

First Edition: April 2015
ISBN - Print: **978-1-940111-16-2**
ISBN - PDF: **978-1-940111-17-9**
ISBN - eEub: **978-1-940111-18-6**
ISBN - Mobi: **978-1-940111-19-3**
ISBN - Safari: **978-1-940111-20-9**

Produced & Printed in the United States

Visit http://www.phparch.com/books/ to purchase additional digital & print copies.

Disclaimer

Written by
John M. Stokes

Published by
musketeers.me, LLC.
201 Adams Ave.
Alexandria, VA 22301
USA
240-348-5PHP (240-348-5747)
info@phparch.com
www.phparch.com

Editor-in-Chief
Oscar Merida

Managing Editor
Eli White

Technical Reviewer
Oscar Merida

Layout and Design
Kevin Bruce

Table of Contents

Chapter 1

Introduction

Why XML?

Extensible Markup Language (XML), like most markup languages, including HTML, descends from Standard General Markup Language (SGML)[1]. XML version 1.0 was formally proposed by the Worldwide Web Consortium (W3C) in February 1998[2] and since then has permeated the online world and been adapted to countless applications.

XML has two major advantages: It is an incredibly flexible format, and it is human readable. XML has very few rules that govern its basic structure. As a result, anyone with a text editor can create a usable XML document with almost no training and because it is human readable, anyone can open an XML document and make some sense out of the data.

[1]   _http://www.w3.org/standards/xml/core_, "What is XML?"
[2]   _http://www.w3.org/XML/hist2002_

The fact that XML is human readable has caused some criticism. To be human readable requires XML to also be verbose, and therefore it isn't the most efficient way to transmit data over a network. Although that's a valid criticism, XML nonetheless retains its popularity because of its understandable, flexible structure, which is easier to pick up and use than are slimmer but more cryptic alternatives such as JSON.

If XML's flexibility was the only aspect of its structure though, it would be very difficult to share XML files between applications. An XML file created for one application may not function in another, as the data structures are different in the two applications. To meet this need for interoperability, the structure of a class of XML documents can be formalized in a number of ways: via a Document Type Definition (DTD), an XML Schema, a schema in Relax NG, and others. Formalizing an XML structure in this way removes some of its flexibility but allows it to be used consistently for a specific task. Examples of formalized XML structures are XHTML, RSS, iCalendar, and MXML.

XML Terminology

The most basic component of an XML document is the *node*. A node is essentially a stopping place in the document, some small section of the document that contains something meaningful. If you imagine climbing a tree, the root node is the trunk, and each branch is another node, a *child* node of the root. Likewise, each branch might have branches coming from it, and they would also be nodes. The climb finally ends at the leaves, which are also nodes. Each node can contain *attributes* (see below), such as "green" for a leaf or "rough" for the bark. (The analogy breaks down somewhat at this point, as attributes are also considered nodes.)

XML documents are constructed by placing data in a number of *elements*. Elements are the most common type of node. Technically, an element consists of a start tag, some content, and an end tag. *Tags* refer to a series of characters or numbers placed inside the angle brackets ‹ and ›. Tags are case sensitive, meaning ‹tag› and ‹TAG› are two different tags. While whiespace is allowed between the brackets, tag identifiers may not contain white space[3]. Collectively, tags are referred to as *markup*[4]. It is common for the term "tag" to informally refer to an entire element rather than a single starting or ending

---

[3]   XML in Theory and Practice, by Chris Bates, p. 19
[4]   *http://www.w3.org/TR/2004/REC-xml11-20040204/#sec-intro*

tag. In this book, we will use the term "element" and "tag" interchangeably unless otherwise noted.

Tags may contain *attributes*, which are key/value pairs that add data to the tag, as in `<book ISBN="12345" author="John Smith"></book>`. "ISBN" and "author" are attributes.

XML may also contain large blocks of non-markup text, called *character data.* Character data is contained in a *CDATA* section[5], which is denoted by the following special tags:

```
`<![CDATA[ Your text goes here ]]>`
```

XML can—and should, for the sake of human readers—contain *comments*, which are notes to a human that a machine parser will ignore. Like HTML, comments are denoted by the special tags `<!-- comment -->`. Unlike HTML, however, XML does not allow an arbitrary number of dashes, as in:

```
<!-----------
-- COMMENT --
------------>
```

Specifically, an XML comment must *end* with only two dashes and a closing angle bracket[6].

Another special tag in XML is the *processing instruction*. Processing instructions are contained between the special tags `<? instruction here ?>`. This should look familiar, as these are also the tags that enclose the XML declaration at the top of most XML files. Although that is the most common processing instruction, there are others.

XML documents are constructed of elements nested within other elements in a hierarchy. That hierarchy is often called a *tree*. An element within another element is referred to as a *child*, with the containing element being the *parent.* Logically, a parent's parents are called *ancestors* and a child's children are called *descendants*. A specific element pruned out of an XML tree with its attributes and value(s) is a *node*. These terms will become extremely familiar through this book.

---

[5]   *http://www.w3.org/TR/2004/REC-xml11-20040204/#sec-cdata-sect*
[6]   *http://www.w3.org/TR/2004/REC-xml11-20040204/#sec-comments*

There are two structural rules you must follow when creating a valid XML document: it must be *well formed*, and it could be *valid*. Being *well formed* is sufficient for many tasks, whereas validation is optional. For an XML document to be *valid*, it must conform to some external validation source, such as a DTD or XML Schema document, which we will discuss in *Chapter 10*.

Even if an XML document has no external validation source, it still must be well formed. Parsers conforming to the XML standard will refuse to parse a document that isn't well formed, instead, returning errors that the document's author can use to correct the document. For an XML document to be well formed[7]:

- It usually starts with an XML declaration: `<?xml version="1.0" encoding="utf-8"?>`. The "encoding" attribute is optional but recommended. This tag may be omitted if the document meets all other well-formed constraints and it is intended to be parsed as XML 1.0. For XML 1.1 and higher, this declaration is required.
- It must have a single, unique root element, which encloses all other elements.
- All elements must be closed, either with a corresponding tag as in `<book></book>` or using shorthand "self-closure" syntax, as in `<book/>`.
- Elements may not be closed out of order. That is, inner "child" elements must be closed before outer "parent" elements, as in `<parent><child></child></parent>`. Thus, the following order is not well formed: `<parent><child></parent></child>`.
- All attributes must be quoted, as in `<book ISBN="12345"/>`. (This is different from HTML.)

Finally, XML has far fewer special characters than HTML does: `&lt;`, `&gt;`, `&amp;`, `&quot;`, and `&apos;` for <, >, &, " and ', respectively. Whereas XML has only these five character entities, an XML document can use any Unicode character by preceding it with `&#`, as in `&#38` (&). Note that the number after `&#` is in decimal, unlike most Unicode tables, which use hexadecimal. XML also understands hexadecimal format of the form `&#x26` (&)[8].

---

[7]   *http://www.w3.org/standards/xml/core*—What is XML Used For?
[8]   *http://www.w3.org/standards/xml/core*—What is XML Used For?

Putting it all together, a well-formed XML document can be as simple as Listing 1.1. For a more complete XML document, see _Appendix D_.

Listing 1.1: Well-formed XML

```
<?xml version="1.0" encoding="UTF-8"?>
<file>
    <filename>example.txt</filename>
    <created>2014-12-11</created>
    <size>1178912</size>
</file>
```

XML Namespaces

Namespaces are a programming concept that is not unique to XML, though few languages use it as frequently. They are a "_space_" in your document in which every _name_ is unique. That alone isn't very exciting: the exciting part comes when you combine namespaces in a single document. Thanks to the namespace, variables with identical names can be differentiated.

To use a classic example, say we have a variable called $orange. If we were writing a drawing program, we'd expect $orange to represent a color. However, if we were writing an e-commerce solution for a grocery store, $orange may well represent a fruit. Take this a step further and imagine that we're writing a grocery e-commerce solution with an integrated photo editor. Whoops! What does $orange mean now?

Enter namespaces.

We can declare a "Color" namespace and populate it with variables such as $orange, $red, $green, and $blue. Then we can declare a "Food" namespace and populate it with $orange, $apple, $milk, and $cheese. This way, we can keep our $orange variables straight by calling them by their namespace.

It doesn't stop there. To add to the melting pot (with a rather far-fetched example), let us imagine that our grocery store has a pharmacy that provides energy supplements for people who feel lethargic and sad. We can declare a "Pharmacy" namespace in which our $blue variable means something completely different from a color. All these variables, and more, can coexist harmoniously in the same document thanks to namespaces.

Let's look at a more practical, real-world example. Here are some excerpts from Adobe's line graph example in Flex's XML-based language, MXML. Full text of this example is available in *Appendix E.*

> *Variable variables are a very powerful tool and should be used with extreme care, not only because they can make your code difficult to understand and document, but also because their improper use can lead to some significant security issues.*

The Flex file starts with an XML declaration and root tag, but they're rather more complicated than those we've seen before.

```
<?xml version="1.0" encoding="utf-8"?>
<s:Application
    xmlns:fx="http://ns.adobe.com/mxml/2009"
    xmlns:s="library://ns.adobe.com/flex/spark"
    xmlns:mx="library://ns.adobe.com/flex/mx">
```

First, there's the familiar <?xml...?> declaration, but our root tag looks unusual. What are all the xmlns:... lines? The prefix xmlns: declares an XML namespace; it is followed immediately by the namespace *prefix*, then an equals sign, and finally, a URL in quotes.

The prefix is used to reference the namespace elsewhere in the document. Note that the prefix cannot stand alone. It must be associated with a URL because it "functions *only* as a placeholder for a namespace name"[9]. Therefore, our root tag is started by the s: prefix, followed by the name of the element as usual. The s: indicates that this particular tag is associated with Adobe's Spark namespace as referenced by the "library:_ns.adobe.com/flex/spark" URL.

The goal of the URL is not necessarily to reference a Document Type Definition or other schema. It is primarily intended to "have the characteristics of uniqueness and persistence"[10]. That is, the URL is meant first and foremost to distinguish itself from other namespaces in the document, though in many cases, it also references a DTD so the document can be validated. In the case of Spark, the Application tag is defined in the DTD and can therefore be validated by its namespace URL in addition to being distinguished by it.

[9]   *http://www.w3.org/TR/REC-xml-names/#ns-qualnames*
[10]   *http://www.w3.org/TR/REC-xml-names/#ns-decl*

Our opening declaration defines two additional namespaces. "mx", which is associated with Macromedia's original MXML definition, now owned by Adobe, and "fx", which is Adobe's reorganization and clarification of some of Macromedia's early code. The "s" prefix refers to Spark, Adobe's next-generation version of MXML.

In the Flex document, each tag is prefixed so the appropriate namespace can be referenced and, if necessary, validated. We've already seen a Spark tag with `<s:Application>`. The Script tag is in the fx namespace and is used for dynamic sections of the document programmed with ActionScript.

```
<fx:Script>
    <![CDATA[
        import mx.collections.ArrayCollection;
        //More ActionScript goes here
    ]]>
</fx:Script>
```

Note that the ActionScript is contained within a CDATA block and is therefore not subject to normal XML text rules.

Finally, older MXML tags that Adobe has not converted to Spark are referenced with the mx prefix.

```
<mx:LineChart id="linechart" height="100%" width="45%"
    paddingLeft="5" paddingRight="5"
    showDataTips="true" dataProvider="{expensesAC}">
    <!-- more tags here -->
</mx:LineChart>
```

Notice that in all the examples, both the opening and closing tags must contain the namespace prefix. Without the prefix, the tags would be meaningless to an application attempting to interpret the document and could cause conflicts, like our two definitions of $orange above. In fact, fx and Spark redefine a number of MXML tags, which, nonetheless, still exist in the MXML library. It is critical to distinguish between the old `<mx:Application>` and `<mx:Script>` tags and the new `<s:Application>` and `<fx:Script>` tags for a Flex application to function. This is true of all XML documents that use namespaces, not just Flex.

The Old Way: DOMXML

PHP 4 provided some XML creation and parsing utilities by means of the
DOMXML library. DOMXML defined a rather cumbersome system of callbacks
in which PHP would walk through an XML file and call a function each time
it encountered what it thought was a tag or other XML feature, as shown in
Listing 1.1.

Listing 1.1 Parsing with DOMXML

```php
<?php
/* Create an XML parser resource */
$parser = xml_parser_create();

/* Define callback functions for the parser
   to handle tags */
xml_set_element_handler($parser,
    'openTagFunction', 'closeTagFunction');

/* Define a callback function to handle CDATA */
xml_set_character_data_handler($parser, 'CDATAfunction');

/* Define other callbacks, for comments, processing
   instructions, etc. here. */

/* Define a callback for the parser to handle anything
   it doesn't understand */
xml_set_default_handler($parser, 'defaultHandler');

function openTagFunction($parser, $element, $attributes) {
    // Handle opening tags...
}

function closeTagFunction($parser, $element) {
    // Handle closing tags
}

function CDATAfunction($parser, $characterData) {
    // Parse CDATA
}
```

That's a great deal of work just to parse a single XML document![11]

---

[11]   Based on example in Programming PHP, 2nd Edition, by Rasmus Lerdorf, Kevin Tatroe, & Peter
        MacIntyre, p.271

In all fairness, DOMXML is more memory efficient because it parses the file one piece at a time, whereas SimpleXML and DOM create representations of the document's entire XML tree. For memory-strapped servers or extremely large XML files, DOMXML is a better option.

The PHP5 Way(s)

PHP 5 introduced several powerful new tools for parsing and creating XML documents, each of which takes full advantage of PHP 5's object-oriented features. SimpleXML and the DOM libraries let you work with fully parsed XML files as objects. However, PHP 5 doesn't leave us completely out in the cold with only memory-hogging parsers. The XMLReader and XMLWriter classes, introduced in PHP 5.1.2, provide a stream-based method of parsing or creating (respectively), XML content, thus giving you, the programmer, more control over caching and memory management. Let's look at them briefly.

SimpleXML

The friendliest of the ways for working with XML in PHP 5 is the SimpleXML library. Though not tremendously powerful, SimpleXML provides tools to handle most common XML parsing and creation tasks and does so, well, simply.

SimpleXML starts with an XML document object, which represents an actual XML document, and provides a handful of logical methods for teasing out aspects of that document, including tags, their values, attribute keys and values, and so on. SimpleXML works best if you have some prior knowledge about the structure of the document you're working with, though it does have some limited self-discovery features.

Creating XML documents with SimpleXML is also straightforward, and simple method calls can construct elements, populate them with values and attributes, and append them to an existing document object. Outputting an XML file constructed in this way requires a single method call, regardless of whether you're displaying from or saving to a file.

DOM

The second major XML library introduced in PHP 5 is the DOM library. Not to be confused with PHP 4's DOMXML library, DOM is a fully object-oriented library that permits you, the programmer, to do almost anything imaginable with an XML document—and a few things you didn't imagine. DOM's power and breadth naturally make it more complicated to use than SimpleXML is, but PHP5 offers the added beauty that DOM objects can be converted to SimpleXML and back again, making it possible to take advantage of SimpleXML's simplicity for mundane tasks while invoking DOM's complexity only when you need its power.

Like SimpleXML, DOM creates an object representing the actual XML document. It covers SimpleXML's methods and provides a myriad of additional methods for accessing and manipulating an XML document. For example, where SimpleXML is limited to adding or changing nodes, DOM can also remove and move nodes. What's more, DOM creates object representations of individual DOM nodes, elements, and attributes so that these can be manipulated directly. Finally, DOM's CDATA and XPath methods are more powerful than are SimpleXML's.

XMLReader and XMLWriter

XMLReader is PHP 5's implementation of an XML pull parser. But what is an XML pull parser? Effectively, an XMLReader object acts as a cursor that walks through your XML document one node at a time. Once you've finished working with a node, you have the option of keeping it or discarding it to free up the memory. Unlike DOMXML, XMLReader doesn't require several callback functions to work. It understands the Document Object Model and traverses your XML document node by node, including all attributes and child nodes, rather than processing each tag or attribute as it encounters them.

XMLWriter works in a similar fashion, constructing an XML document as a stream: creating opening tags and attributes and closing tags individually and then sending them on their merry way down the yellow brick output stream (be it a file or network stream) as it finishes with them. This makes it more memory efficient than is SimpleXML or DOM. This does require a bit more care on the programmer's part, as you don't have the flexibility to later jump back to, for example, the second node and add that attribute you forgot the first time.

The Road Ahead

In addition to an in-depth discussion of parsing and creating XML documents with SimpleXML, DOM, and XMLReader/XMLWriter, we will discuss a few other XML-related technologies, such as XPath and StAX. XPath is a powerful query language that allows us to zero in on pieces of an XML document that we care about when browsing or when more generalized search functions aren't enough. StAX (not to be confused with SAX) is the "pull" approach to parsing XML used by XMLReader. We'll also provide an overview of popular uses of XML in the wild, such as RSS.

Chapter 2

Introduction to XPath

What is XPath?

Officially, XPath is a "query language" for XML. Let's clarify exactly what that mean.

XPath is a sometimes cryptic string of characters we can use to search and extract data from XML documents with a great deal of specificity. If you are familiar with regular expressions, XPath is similar in concept—*though not in syntax*—in that you can build up powerful queries by putting together path expressions. This chapter introduces XPath concepts, although we won't see how they look in PHP code until later chapters.

XPath is short for XML Path Language and was originally recommended by the W3C on November 16, 1999[1]. It has since been revised, and the recommendation for XPath 2.0 was formalized December 14, 2010[2]. Much of SimpleXML and DOM were created before XPath 2.0 was, so this book will focus on version 1.0. XPath is designed to provide a universal syntax for navigating through any XML document[3]. A developer doesn't need to know details about the structure of a specific XML document to use XPath effectively. As such, it forms the basis for a number of other XML-related technologies, such as XSLT, that are beyond the scope of this book.

XPath treats XML documents, or portions of documents, as a tree of nodes (see Chapter 1 if you need a refresher on nodes.) XPath *expressions*—that sometimes cryptic string of characters—are usually relative to a given node in an XML document, called the *context node*[4]. The context node does not need to be the root. A single XPath expression can start with the root node as its context node, dig three levels deep in the document, set a new context node there, and then be run again to take you deeper.

XPath Expressions

In their simplest, and longest, form, XPath expressions resemble a file path on your computer. Expressions are typically aimed at finding a specific location in the document—that is, a specific node and its descendants. These types of expressions are called *location paths*[5]. Like paths in your computer's file system, location paths can be absolute or relative. Absolute paths start with a forward slash / followed by the name of the root node, whereas relative paths start with the name of an arbitrary node in the document. Additional elements in an XPath expression are also separated by forward slashes.

Using our `library.xml` file from *Appendix D*, a query for the entire document would look like... wait for it...

```
/library
```

The leading slash indicates that this is an absolute path expression. Retrieving the entire document though isn't generally very useful. We can build on this, for example, to retrieve all "book" nodes by adding to that expression.

[1]   http://www.w3.org/TR/xpath/
[2]   http://www.w3.org/TR/xpath20/
[3]   XML in Theory and Practice, by Chris Bates, p. 140
[4]   XML in Theory and Practice, by Chris Bates, p. 142
[5]   XML in Theory and Practice, by Chris Bates, p. 143

```
/library/book
```

This gets us a list filled with nodes representing each book. Now we can loop through it and do something with those book nodes. That's still not terribly exciting though, is it? What if, instead, we wanted to retrieve all our book titles without needing to loop through every node?

```
book/title
```

Even though `<title>` elements are children of `<book>` elements, XPath will find them. This query gives us a list of `<title>` nodes, without spurious details such as author and publisher mucking it up.

Note also that we omitted the leading slash and `library`. Our XPath query reads `book/title`, not `/library/book/title`. This is therefore a relative path, as I mentioned above. Because we provided no context node, the context node is set to the root node by default, so the two queries are equivalent. We'll play more with relative queries later.

For our official records, we also need the ISBN number of each book, but that's contained in an attribute. We can get to attributes by preceding our node name with the @ sign.

```
/library/book/@ISBN
```

Because nearly everything in an XML document is a node, this gives us a list that we can loop through just like our titles.

Another aspect of attribute-related syntax is worth mentioning. Consider this query:

```
/library/book[@ISBN]
```

This doesn't give us the value of ISBN attributes; rather, it gives us every book node that *has* an ISBN attribute.

XPath Predicates

XPath actually allows us to query specific nodes in a list with syntax very similar to PHP's array notation:

```
/library/book[1]/title
```

Identifiers tacked on to the end of an item in an XPath query are called *predicates*. Before we look at more predicates, however, notice that something very important happened in that last XPath query. Did you see it? We retrieved our first book node with the number 1, not 0 as in native PHP. XPath counts starting from one, which we PHP programmers must remember.

> *To further muddy the waters, several versions of Internet Explorer count from 0 in spite of the W3C recommendation. This shouldn't be a concern if you're executing server-side PHP, but beware of anything executing client side!*

That disclaimer made, let's return to predicates. We've already seen a number in brackets. Technically, the book[@ISBN] we saw above is also a predicate. A predicate is always contained in brackets after a node name. A useful extension to the attribute predicate is querying for a specific attribute.

```
book[@ISBN="NA"]
```

@ISBN="NA" returns only those books with an ISBN attribute of NA. XPath also includes some predicate functions.

```
book[last()]
```

Predictably, this returns the last book. We can also perform simple math with the results of these functions.

```
book[last() - 1]
```

This returns the next-to-last book. Consider also:

```
book[position() = 4]
```

This returns the fourth book because XPath starts counting at one. Another useful thing we can do with the position() function is:

```
book[position() < 4]
```

This returns the first three books. We can also search for specific elements contained in a node, not just attributes. Say we wanted all books published recently.

```
book[year > 1999]
```

Notice that, to access elements rather than attributes, we simply omit the @ inside the brackets. As you might expect, you can extend the query past any of these predicates just as we did above with the number in brackets, so a query like this is perfectly legal:

```
book[position() < 4]/title
```

XPath Shortcuts

We've looked at many XPath queries but, so far, they've relied on our knowledge of the document and have been rather cumbersome. Imagine if we had a large library with a great many subject areas and multimedia, such as videos, for example. To get titles, we'd need to construct a number of queries like these:

```
/library/book/nonfiction/geography/Africa/title
/library/video/geography/Africa/title
/library/book/nonfiction/geography/Asia/title
/library/video/geography/Asia/title
 etc.
```

XPath seems to just make things more difficult! Fortunately, there's an easier way. We can, instead, get all our titles with this simple query:

```
//title
```

The double slash // tells XPath to "find this node no matter where it is." Suppose we only want book titles returned. We can use a similar query to tell XPath to ignore videos and other media types.

```
book//title
```

A node name followed by double slashes and another node name tells XPath to find all descendants of a node type. Specifically, this tells XPath to find all <title> nodes that are descendants of <book> nodes but to ignore titles of all other node types, like our hypothetical <video> nodes.

Earlier, we found all our ISBN attributes by specifying the path to our ISBN attributes with /library/book/@ISBN. That query, unfortunately, will create the same problem we saw above in our extensive modern library. However, we can combine the // shortcut with the @ symbol to shorten this.

```
//@ISBN
```

This will find all ISBN attributes wherever they are in our document. However, ISBN attributes alone aren't that useful. It would be best to combine them with book titles.

```
book_@ISBN | book_title
```

The pipe symbol | allows us to combine XPath queries together.

XPath also provides wildcards, which should look familiar; ∗ and @∗ select all elements and attributes, respectively. This is how XPath allows a program to self-discover and parse a document when its structure is unknown.

Can we select every node though, regardless of type? There isn't a wildcard for that, but XPath provides a function: node().

As with other XPath shortcuts, wildcards can be combined with other expressions.

```
book[@ISBN="NA"]/∗
```

This query returns all details about every public domain book.

XPath Axes

One more XPath concept we should discuss is that of XPath axes. "Axes" is just a fancy term for the XPath family tree. Axes take on such names as "ancestor", "child", and "descendant" and are a means of accessing node lists relative to the current node.

An axes precedes a node name in XPath queries and is separated from that node name by double colons: ::. Let's suppose we have a context node of <title> and we want to back up and get all book nodes.

```
ancestor::book
```

That's not especially interesting in our small library, but for larger documents, it adds yet another option to our self-discovery and parsing powers.

The table below lists helpful XPath axes in order of depth[6].

Axes	Description
ancestor	All nodes that are ancestors (parent, grandparents, etc.) of the current node
ancestor-or-self	All ancestor nodes plus the current node
parent	The immediate parent of the current node
preceding	The entire document prior to the current node's opening tag
preceding-sibling	All siblings (nodes at the same depth) prior to the current node
self	The current node
following-sibling	All siblings after the current node
following	The entire document after the current node's closing tag
child	All immediate children of the current node
descendant-or-self	All descendants (children, grandchildren, etc.) of the current node, plus the current node itself
descendant	All descendants of the current node

There are a few other XPath axes not directly related to a node's depth.

- **attribute** — All attributes of the current node
- **namespace** — All namespaces that apply to the current node (See *Chapter 6*)

Axes can be combined with shortcut expressions just like more generic expressions.

```
child::*
descendant::text()
```

[6]   Based on *http://www.w3schools.com/xpath/xpath_axes.asp*

Summary

This chapter is by no means a comprehensive look at XPath, but it should give you a solid understanding of some of the most common XPath queries. We've seen normal query syntax, how to use context nodes in PHP, and how to shorten that syntax with XPath shortcuts. We will revisit XPath with PHP code examples in the chapters to come.

Chapter 3

Basic SimpleXML

Parsing with SimpleXML

Occasionally users, and even programmers, are confused by the word *parsing*. It just means "getting meaning from data." When you see **THE**, it's the difference between *seeing* a cross, a goalpost, and a one-sided ladder and *reading* the word "the". So when we speak of "parsing" an XML file, we mean we're going to load the data and do something meaningful with it instead of just echoing it back to the screen unchanged.

In my experience, reading and manipulating data occur much more often than writing it does. Consequently, we'll start by examining how to do just that. Fortunately, reading and doing simple manipulations are where SimpleXML excels.

Almost every SimpleXML object is instantiated by importing a well-formed XML document, either from a file on disk or a preexisting string. You have two options for doing so: procedural and object oriented. Either way, you end up with a SimpleXML object that you can manipulate using its built-in methods.

Because the only stand-alone procedures in the SimpleXML library relate to importing XML data, whereas all others are method calls against objects, it seems logical to start your SimpleXML work in an object-oriented fashion, with the new operator. I will demonstrate the procedural approaches in this section, but all other examples in the book will use the object-oriented approach.

All examples in this book will use the library.xml file from *Appendix D*.

Loading from a File

Many times, you'll be parsing an XML file on disk created by another application or perhaps by yourself in the past. To do so, call simplexml_load_file() as follows (of course the path may differ depending on where you save it locally):

```
$library = simplexml_load_file('library.xml');
```

No, it really is that simple. We now have a lovely SimpleXML object called $library waiting to be manipulated.

The object-oriented approach is slightly more confusing than the procedural one is, as the new operator assumes you're loading a string rather than a file path. Therefore, we need to pass in a couple of extra parameters: $data, $options, and $data_is_url.

Before I show you the syntax, let's discuss these parameters: $data is, in the case of loading a file from disk, just a file path. $options is where you can specify a number of Libxml parameters, as specified in Appendix D. For now, we'll just set that to zero. $data_is_url is where the magic happens. It defaults to FALSE, but we'll set it to TRUE to let the constructor know that $data is actually a file path rather than an XML string. As the variable name suggests, $data could be a URL, such as from an RSS feed, or a file path on the local disk.

> *To use a URL to load an XML string, you need to ensure* `allow_url_fopen` *is set to On in your* `php.ini` *configuration file.*

```
$library = new SimpleXMLElement('library.xml', 0, true);
```

We now have a SimpleXML object identical to the one `simplexml_load_file()` gave us.

You might be wondering why the class is called `SimpleXMLElement`. Remember our discussion of XML elements in Chapter 1? "Element" is the name for anything in an XML document that's surrounded by tags. A SimpleXMLElement object then can represent any element with all its sub-elements, from a single `<author>` element with no children to the entire `<library>` hierarchy. This concept of an object representing the whole tree or any subsection of the tree becomes especially important when we examine DOM.

Loading from a String

If you already have an XML string loaded into a variable, perhaps from a database or an Internet feed, you can convert that to a SimpleXML object in a similar manner to loading from a file.

The procedural approach involves passing the string to a function. Let's assume we have a function that loads XML from a database and returns it as a string:

```
$libString = loadXMLfromDatabase();
```

We can turn that string into a SimpleXML object procedurally with this call:

```
$library = simplexml_load_string($libString);
```

Just like that, we have a SimpleXML object.

The object-oriented approach is just as simple. Because we're loading from a string, we can rely on defaults for the other parameters and omit them.

```
$library = new SimpleXMLElement($libString);
```

Accessing Data

XML data is generally contained in either the content of an element or an attribute. Both are easily accessible through SimpleXML using PHP's familiar object or array notation.

Let's start by retrieving child elements from the parent element we just created using SimpleXML's children() method. This is usually done in a loop.

```
foreach ($library->children() as $book) {
    echo $book->title . "\n";
}
```

The children() method does not actually return an array. Rather, it returns an *object that implements the Traversable interface.* That is, it returns an object that can be looped (iterated) over and therefore used with any iterative construct. Let's do the same thing with a for loop:

```
$count = $library->count();
for ($i=0; $i<$count; $i++) {
    echo $library->book[$i]->title . "\n";
}
```

SimpleXML's count() method gives us the number of children under the current element. As you can probably guess, a while loop with a counter will also work. But be warned! count() only works with PHP 5.3.0 or higher.

> *If you're wondering why I put $library->count() into a variable instead of just putting it in the for() loop directly, that's considered a best practice. Putting the length in a variable saves PHP from recalculating it every time it iterates over the for() loop and thereby speeds up your application.*

Which loop approach is preferable? There's no practical difference. When foreach iterates over objects, they are passed by reference, so you can modify and manipulate them just as in a for loop.

If you already know the structure of your XML document and thus also know exactly which element you need, you can access it directly. For example:

```
echo $library->book[2]->author;
// Prints Lewis Carroll
```

What about those attributes? We can access them in a similar manner.

```
foreach ($library->children() as $book) {
    echo $book['ISBN'];
}
```

Attributes are accessed with array-style notation. As such, we can jump directly to the attribute we want with multidimensional array notation:

```
echo $library->book[4]['ISBN'];
//Prints 0765328321
```

What if we don't know the name of our elements or attributes? SimpleXML introduced the getName() method in PHP 5.1.3 for that purpose[1]. getName() works with both elements and attributes. Let's assume we've extracted a specific book node from our library:

```
foreach ($book->children() as $child) {
    echo $child->getName() . "\n";
    //Prints title, then author, etc.
}
foreach ($book->attributes() as $attr) {
    echo $attr->getName() . "\n";
    //Prints ISBN
}
```

Notice the attributes() method we used on the child node. If an XML element has one or more attributes, you can use attributes() to loop through them in the same manner we used children() to loop through child nodes.

We mentioned in *Chapter 1* that XML has very few special characters. So what happens if an XML tag has a character that's illegal in PHP? Those can be accessed in a similar manner to quoted array values: by placing them within curly braces. For example, say another XML file for books used two tags for author names: <author-first-name> and <author-last-name>:

```
<?xml version="1.0" encoding="utf-8"?>
<authors>
    <author>
        <author-first-name>Lewis</author-first-name>
        <author-last-name>Carroll</author-last-name>
    </author>
</author>
```

[1] php[architect]'s *Zend PHP 5 Certification Study Guide, 3rd edition*, by Davey Shafik and Ben Ramsey, p. 198

The hyphen isn't allowed in PHP identifiers, so to access it, we use this syntax:

```
echo $library->book[0]->{'author-first-name'},
     ' ', $library->book[0]->{'author-last-name'};
// Prints Jane Austen
```

What about those CDATA elements? Before we move on from basic parsing, we had better tackle those. As it happens, there is little to tackle. CDATA fields are returned exactly like a normal field is, so we can access an excerpt of Mr. Conan Doyle's book this way:

```
echo $library->book[1]->excerpt;
```

Creating with SimpleXML

You'll spend a good deal of your XML programming time on parsing, but that's only half the picture. At some point, you'll need to create XML documents programmatically.

You could construct an XML document out of raw strings, without the help of any library. In fact, for small documents with a simple structure, that approach will likely be the easiest one. We'll look at an example of just that in Listing 9.9 in *Chapter 9*. Once the hierarchy gets more than a few nodes deep though, you'll probably want some help keeping track of it all and ensuring that the resulting XML document is well formed.

SimpleXML can help. Unlike DOM, SimpleXML is not able to create XML documents from nothing. At a bare minimum, you'll need to create an empty XML document that looks something like this:

```
<?xml version="1.0" encoding="utf-8"?>
<root>
</root>
```

You can then pass that document to SimpleXML's constructor or one of the load_() functions to effectively create an empty SimpleXML object.

```
$string = '<?xml version="1.0" encoding="utf-8"?>
<root>
</root>';

// using the constructor
$xml = new SimpleXMLElement($string);

// loading the string
$xml = simplexml_load_string($string);
```

Whether you start with an empty XML document or a larger document, SimpleXML allows you to change values and add nodes.

Changing elements and their attributes follows the variable format that is exactly like our parsing examples above. To change the contents of a tag or attribute, simply assign new values to it with the equals sign.

```
$library->book[0]->publisher = 'Tribeca Books';
$library->book[0]->year = 2011;
$library->book[0]['ISBN'] = 1612930425;
```

Adding new nodes to a SimpleXML object is accomplished with the addChild() method. addChild() works with a key/value pair, with the value being optional, and returns the node it just created. Therefore, we can add a "book" element as a key without any value, receive the book node object back, and populate the new book element with additional key/value pairs:

```
$newBook = $library->addChild('book');
$newBook->addChild('title', 'Mass Effect: Revelation');
$newBook->addChild('author', 'Drew Karpyshyn');
```

But wait! Doesn't our book need an ISBN attribute, too? Predictably, we can populate that with a similar key/value pair using the addAttribute() method. Unlike addChild(), the value parameter is required.

```
$newBook->addAttribute('ISBN', '034549816X');
```

Returning to XML

So we've parsed an XML document, edited it, and added to it. Now we're ready to return it to disk or screen as XML. How do we squeeze raw XML out of our fancy SimpleXML object? To return your object as a string of well-formed XML, use the asXML() method. If, however, you want to write your object to disk, you'd use the asXML() method. That's right, SimpleXML's powerful little asXML() method can either return your object as a string or manage all the file I/O to write it to disk. It makes the distinction simply by whether or not we pass in a file path, with no messy Booleans or nulls required.

To return our XML as a string:

```
echo $library->asXML();
```

Or to write it to disk:

```
$library->asXML('NewLibrary.xml');
```

The Road Ahead

We've learned three approaches to creating SimpleXML objects, how to access elements and attributes with object and variable notation or with the children() and attributes() methods, how to modify elements and attributes with object and variable notation, and how to add to the object with addChild() and addAttribute(). When we've finished with our SimpleXML processing, we output it as raw XML with the asXML() method. Not too painful, right? Let's take it up another notch in the next chapter with some advanced SimpleXML.

Chapter 4

Advanced SimpleXML

Most of SimpleXML's advanced features relate to namespaces, discussed in _Chapter 1_

Namespaces in SimpleXML

Parsing with Namespaces

Let's load the Flex document in _Appendix E_ and create a SimpleXML object with it. Recall from _Chapter 2_ that we can do this two ways: by loading the data first and then passing it to SimpleXML or by loading directly with `simplexml_load_file()`.

```php
//Load the file into a variable first
$FlexDoc = file_get_contents('FlexDoc.xml');
$mxml = new SimpleXMLElement($FlexDoc);

//OR
//Load the file directly
$mxml = simplexml_load_file('FlexDoc.xml');
```

Most of SimpleXML's functions accept a $namespace variable, including the constructor, children() and attribute() functions. Setting $namespace and $is_prefix in the constructor sets the XML namespace to iterate over by default. The children() method requires a namespace parameter to return the elements specified in a particular namespace. For example, if we want the fx namespace elements with the children() function, we must access them this way:

```
foreach ($mxml->children('fx', true) as $child) {
    echo $child->asXML();
}
//Prints <fx:Script></fx:Script> and its contents
```

The children() call specified the namespace prefix "fx" followed by a Boolean true. The Boolean specifies whether the namespace passed in the first parameter is a namespace URL or a namespace prefix and defaults to false, indicating it expects a URL. As such, we could access the same data by passing the fully qualified URL to the children() call and eliminate the Boolean because it defaults to false.

```
$FlexDoc = file_get_contents('FlexDoc.xml');
$mxml = new SimpleXMLElement($FlexDoc);
$mxml_ns = 'http://ns.adobe.com/mxml/2009'
foreach ($mxml->children($mxml_ns) as $child) {
    echo $child->asXML();
}
//Prints <fx:Script></fx:Script> and its contents
```

You might expect that leaving the children() method call empty would return the entire document. Unfortunately, that's not the case. children() with no parameters returns only those nodes that are *not* namespace qualified. In the case of our MXML document, it returns nothing. To access the entire document, we must make three separate calls:

```
$spark = $mxml->children('s', true);
$fx = $mxml->children('fx', true);
$mx = $mxml->children('mx', true);
```

What if we don't know all the namespaces in the document? SimpleXML provides some basic self-discovery features for unknown namespaces.

getNamespaces() returns all namespaces used in a document. It takes an optional Boolean argument which, if set to true, will recursively search the document for every namespace used. So we can get namespaces used in our MXML document this way:

```
$ns = $mxml->getNamespaces();
var_dump($ns);
```

Prints:

```
array(1) {
    ["s"]=>string(33) "library:_ns.adobe.com/flex/spark"
}
```

Wait a moment! We have three namespaces in our document, why did getNamespaces() return only one? One key to remember is that getNamespaces() returns only those namespaces that *are used* in the document. Because we didn't recursively search the entire document, getNamespaces() searched only the root node, and the only namespace *used* in the root node is the "s" namespace. We could pass a Boolean true (ex: $mxml->getNamespaces(true);) to recursively search the document, but for a large document, that would be quite resource intensive, and we have a better way.

getDocNamespaces() returns all namespaces *declared* in the document. Thus, by doing the same process above, we have:

```
$ns = $mxml->getDocNamespaces();
var_dump($ns);
```

Which prints out the following:

```
array(3) {
    ["fx"]=>string(29) "http://ns.adobe.com/mxml/2009"
    ["s"]=>string(33) "library://ns.adobe.com/flex/spark"
    ["mx"]=>string(30) "library://ns.adobe.com/flex/mx"
}
```

Like getNamespaces(), getDocNamespaces() accepts a Boolean to tell it whether to recursively search the whole document. Because it is possible to declare namespaces later in a document, this might be necessary. However, the convention is to declare your namespaces at the top of a document, so a lightweight call to getDocNamespaces(), without passing in true, will typically prove most useful for your day-to-day parsing.

Putting it all together, we can parse our entire document this way:

```
$ns = $mxml->getDocNamespaces();
foreach ($ns as $namespace) {
    foreach ($mxml->children($namespace) as $child) {
        echo $child->asXML() . "<br />\n";
    }
}
```

Notice that I didn't pass `true` to the `$s->children()` call. The array values `getDocNamespaces()` returns are URLs, not prefixes. We could access the prefixes by dereferencing both the key and value in our `foreach()` statement.

```
foreach ($ns as $prefix=>$namespace) {
    foreach ($mxml->children($prefix, true) as $child) {
        echo $child->asXML() . "<br />\n";
    }
}
```

XPath

It's time to take those concepts we introduced in _Chapter 2_ and put them to practical use. SimpleXML provides limited XPath support. XPath query results are returned as an array of SimpleXMLElement objects. Those objects can then be accessed with array and object style notation as discussed in _Chapter 3_. SimpleXML provides only one method for employing XPath: the prosaically named `xpath()` method. To execute an XPath expression, simply pass the expression as a string to `xpath()`.

```
$bookList = $SimpleXMLdoc->xpath('/library/book');
foreach ($bookList as $book) {
    echo $book->title . "\n";
}
```

Note that SimpleXML's `xpath()` method offers no support for context nodes. All queries are run relative to the root node, so a query like the one below will return no results.

```
$titles = $SimpleXMLdoc->xpath('title'); //Returns nothing
```

Let's try parsing a different way. Suppose I already know the namespace and node I want. I can jump directly to it with XPath.

```
$chart = $mxml->xpath('/s:Application/mx:Panel/mx:LineChart');
foreach ($chart[0]->attributes() as $attr) {
    $attrName = $attr->getName();
    echo $attrName . ': '
        . $chart[0][$attrName] . "<br />\n";
}
//Prints id: LineChart<br />, etc.
```

Notice I included the prefixes in the XPath query. Suppose we have a large block of tags we want to work with and a rather lengthy prefix. We can shorten that prefix with registerXPathNamespace(). For example, all the details of our LineChart and its sub-tags are in the "mx" namespace, but we can shorten that to "m" with the call below. This has the added benefit of "locking in" that prefix for our following XPath calls, so even if the XML document's author adds an "m" prefix in the future, XPath will still understand which "m" namespace we mean.

```
$mxml->registerXPathNamespace(
    'm', 'library://ns.adobe.com/flex/mx'
);
$chart = $mxml->xpath('m:LineChart');
```

All subsequent XPath calls will understand that the "m" namespace refers to the URL "library://ns.adobe.com/flex/mx", regardless of how the source document might change.

The attributes() method also accepts a namespace parameter, but that is only useful in the rare scenario of specifying attributes in namespaces other than its parent tag, for example, if you had a tag that looked like this:

```
<fx:Declarations mx:id="declarationsBlock">
```

Most of the time, tags are namespaced and attributes are not. You may rarely need to pass a namespace parameter to attributes().

Creating with Namespaces

Like parsing, creating with namespaces uses the same methods we learned in *Chapter 2* but with additional namespace parameters. Let us assume we have a SimpleXML object with the XML, root tag, and namespace declaration above. We'll start by adding the `<fx:Script>` tag.

```
$ActionScript = 'import mx.collections.ArrayCollection;';
$mxml->addChild(
    'Script', $ActionScript, 'http://ns.adobe.com/mxml/2009'
);
```

By passing in the namespace as the third parameter, SimpleXML will correctly resolve the namespace and apply the prefix to our Script tag. Unfortunately, `addChild()` doesn't support a fourth `$is_prefix` Boolean parameter, so we must pass the namespace as a URL. What if we were to save a step and pass the prefix as part of the tag name?

```
$mxml->addChild('fx:Script', $ActionScript);
//Creates an <s:Script></s:Script> tag
```

That didn't work. SimpleXML strips the prefix and puts the tag in the default context without the URL, so we are forced to use the three-parameter method call.

Passing a prefix as the third parameter to `addChild()` creates a completely different problem: SimpleXML thinks you're declaring a new namespace and will add an `xmlns` attribute to your tag, even if the prefix is already defined in your document.

```
$mxml->addChild('Script', $ActionScript, 'fx');
//Creates a <Script xmlns="fx"></Script> tag.
```

Therefore, when using `add...()` methods, remember to keep your namespace URLs handy.

The code above creates another problem for us, specifically with the `$ActionScript` variable. Can you guess it? The `<fx:Script>` tag needs a CDATA block, but I didn't add the CDATA tags to my `$ActionScript` variable. Believe it or not, that was intentional. `addChild()` will automatically change any special characters to their entity equivalents. Instead of getting `<![CDATA[ ]]>` tags, we'd get `&lt;![CDATA[ ]]&gt;`.

This is a problem that can only be solved with DOM, which leads us to our next topic.

Loading from DOM

Both SimpleXML and DOM provide a procedure that converts an object to one of the other types. Converting between the two is a simple matter of passing the object of one type to the appropriate function. To convert our SimpleXML object to DOM in order to create our CDATA node, we use `dom_import_simplexml()`:

```
$DOMobj = dom_import_simplexml($mxml);
```

Now we can add our `$ActionScript` CDATA section correctly. Note that I am omitting the `<![CDATA[ ]]>` tags, as in the original variable.

```
$ActionScriptCDATA = new DOMCdataSection($ActionScript);
$ActionScriptNode = new DOMElement(
    'fx:Script', null, 'http://ns.adobe.com/mxml/2009'
);
$DOMobj->appendChild($ActionScriptNode);
$ActionScriptNode->appendChild($ActionScriptCDATA);
```

That example may look a little intimidating right now, but we will cover this in more depth in *Chapter 6*.

Finally, we can convert the DOM object back to SimpleXML to continue our simple processing.

```
$mxml = simplexml_import_dom($DOMobj);
```

It really is that easy.

The Road Ahead

If you've been reading this book straight through, you should now have a practical understanding of most XML concepts, including such advanced topics as XPath and namespaces. In the next chapter, we'll tackle the same tasks with a slightly more complicated but considerably more powerful library. Onward to DOM!

Chapter
5

Basic DOM

Parsing with DOM

SimpleXML, in keeping with its theme of simplicity, has all its methods contained in a single class. Not so with DOM. DOM is a class hierarchy that represents XML documents, nodes, elements, and attributes with separate classes, as you can see in Figure 5.1. Many of the classes inherit from DOMNode, so you'll see several references to that class throughout the chapter. For now, let's start at the beginning: how does an XML document become a DOMDocument object?

Figure 5.1: DOM Class Hierarchy

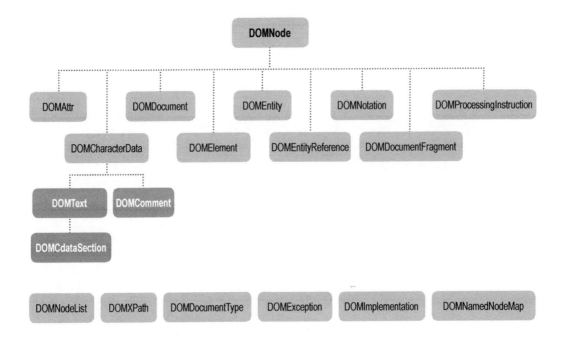

Loading XML

Like SimpleXML, DOM is nearly completely object oriented. Unlike SimpleXML, however, there are no stand-alone functions for loading XML documents from a string or file. To create a DOM object, you must always invoke the DOMDocument class's constructor with the new operator.

```
$DOMdoc = new DOMDocument();
```

That looks rather different from SimpleXML. Where do we pass the file path to XML data on disk? How do we pass in an XML string? Rather than handling that in the constructor, DOM has dedicated methods to load XML data from a variety of sources.

DOM is not restricted to loading well-formed XML. It provides two methods for loading files: load( ), which expects a file path to a well-formed XML document, and loadHTML( ), which expects a file path to an HTML file. loadHTML( ) does not require that the document be well-formed XHTML—any HTML file will do. Be prepared for DOM to complain—the dirtier the HTML, the more warnings will be generated. Once the grumbling is over though, you will have a viable DOMDocument object. Note also that loadHTML( ) does not take the DTD into account, and therefore the document can't be validated. More on that in *Chapter 10*.

Lest I bore you with more details, let's import our library:

```
$DOMdoc->load('library.xml');
```

Naturally, we can also create a DOMDocument from an XML string that we've already loaded from a database or some other source, but doing so requires a separate method instead of toggling some parameters in the load() method. Like Chapter 3, let's imagine we have a function that loads XML from a database and returns it as a string:

```
$libString = loadXMLfromDatabase();
```

We can produce a DOMDocument from that string with the loadXML() method:

```
$DOMdoc->loadXML($libString);
```

I mentioned above that DOM can work with HTML documents that are not well-formed XML. While we're imagining, let's imagine for a moment that my library is, in fact, a web page rather than an XML document. I can create a DOMDocument object directly from the web page code with loadHTMLFile().

```
$DOMdoc->loadHTMLFile('library.html');
```

Not surprisingly, loadHTMLFile() has a sister function for loading HTML from a string, loadHTML();

```
$libString = loadHTMLfromDatabase();
$DOMdoc->loadHTML($libString);
```

The names of these four methods are easy to confuse, as loading XML from a file has the simple load() method name, whereas loading HTML has the rather pedantic name loadHTMLFile(). A useful memory aid is to remember the load<Something> methods, loadXML() and loadHTML(), both refer to loading string variables.

Accessing Data

Once you have XML data loaded into a DOMDocument object, DOM offers a number of ways to access it. Elements and attributes are both represented by their own objects. DOM relies heavily on the XPath query language for self-discovery and parsing. We will see DOM's use of XPath in detail in *Chapter 6*.

For the purposes of this discussion, let's assume we have a solid idea of what our XML data looks like.

We can extract XML nodes by a method reminiscent of JavaScript: getElementsByTagName(). Predictably, this method returns all the elements that match the passed tag. Like SimpleXML's children() method, getElementsByTagName() returns an iterative object rather than an array. Specifically, it returns a DOMNodeList.

DOMNodeList is a simple class that defines only a length parameter and an item() method. These tools allow us to loop through our list of nodes with a for() or while() loop.

```
$bookList = $DOMdoc->getElementsByTagName('book');
//$bookList is a DOMNodeList object
for ($i=0; $i < $bookList->length; $i++) {
    echo $bookList->item($i)->nodeValue;
}
```

Because a DOMNodeList is a Traversable object, it actually can be traversed by a foreach loop as well.

```
foreach ($bookList as $book) {
    echo $book->nodeValue;
}
```

In the example above, we know $book inherits from DOMNode because it is extracted from the DOMNodeList object, $bookList. Therefore, we can access the nodeValue property. More on that in a moment.

You can extract a single XML node with another method familiar to JavaScript programmers: getElementById(). Like JavaScript, getElementById() retrieves a specific element and its children by searching the document for a matching id attribute. However, there's a catch. Unlike HTML, XML does not require the node's unique identifier to be named id, so we can't simply call getElementById("<id name>"). First, we have to tell DOM which attribute is the ID for each node. We can do so by looping through the $bookList we extracted above.

```
foreach ($bookList as $book) {
    $book->setIdAttribute('id', true);
}
```

Because id is a logical name for our ID attribute, we loop through each node and set the ID attribute to be id. Passing true as the second parameter tells DOM that the name we're passing is, in fact, the ID attribute. We can unset the ID attribute by passing false. Now that DOM knows where to look for the name of our ID, we can extract a single element.

```
$bookNode = $DOMdoc->getElementById('B4');
```

That call will create a DOMElement object with all the data from *A Christmas Carol*. Of course that raises the question, "What do we do with a DOMElement object"?

The DOMNode class, from which DOMElement inherits, defines a childNodes property very similar to SimpleXML's children() method. The childNodes property is actually a DOMNodeList object. Other useful properties for hopping about within your DOMElement object are firstChild, lastChild, previousSibling, and nextSibling, which do exactly what their names suggest. Thus, we could access the author of *A Christmas Carol* in the following manner:

```
echo $bookNode->firstChild->nextSibling->nextSibling
            ->nextSibling->nodeValue;
//Prints Charles Dickens
```

The nodeValue property is also defined in the DOMNode class, so it is available to any object that inherits from that class, including DOMElement and DOMAttr. But why are there so many nextSibling calls? In a minified XML document, we could have skipped a couple of those, but in a nicely formatted, readable document, the spaces between nodes are themselves empty text nodes, so we have to traverse them as well. You can dig through the clutter to find the node you want with the nodeName property.

For our final XML parsing function, we'll depart from the familiar land of JavaScript to discover a uniquely XML method: getAttribute(). getAttribute() returns the value for a key passed to the method. So returning to our $bookNode by the author above, we can get the ISBN number as follows:

```
echo $bookNode->getAttribute('ISBN');
//Prints NA
```

Unlike most of the methods we've discussed thus far, getAttribute() is not defined in DOMNode. Rather, it is from the DOMElement class. If you think about it, this makes sense. DOMAttr also inherits from DOMNode, and attributes can not contain other attributes, so defining it in DOMNode would add the overhead of useless methods.

Creating with DOM

Because DOM is a class hierarchy, the process for creating an XML document with DOM is to create objects of the appropriate class and then add them to other objects in increasing detail until you can finally add them to the DOMDocument object itself.

This is why DOM doesn't require you to pass XML data in the constructor. It is entirely possible you'll want to start with a blank document and build your XML document programmatically with DOM's help.

To add a book to our library, we'll perform these basic workflow steps:

1. Create DOMElement objects for the title, author, and so on.
2. Create a DOMAttr object for the ISBN
3. Create a DOMElement object for the book
4. Insert the title, author, etc., objects into the book object
5. Insert the ISBN object into the book object
6. Insert the book object into the DOMDocument object

I prefer to work from the "inside out." That is, I start with the most specific, and therefore most deeply nested, part of the hierarchy and create objects of less and less specificity until I emerge at the root object: The DOMDocument. Because it's more difficult to add incomplete nodes to the document and fill them in later, I find this approach helps me keep track of where I am in the construction of my document and ensures I have all the child nodes, attributes, CDATA sections, and the like assembled before I insert their parent node into the document. This is by no means the only approach though. If you find it "backward" or stifling your coding style, find an approach that works for you.

That said, let's move ahead with creating the DOMElement objects that detail our new book node.

Object construction can be done in traditional object-oriented fashion with the new operator or via the DOMDocument instance. However, calling one of DOMDocument's create...( ) methods does just that—create—and nothing else. Regardless of the approach you choose, the entities still must be added to the document.

```
$DOMdoc = new DOMDocument();

// Calling DOMElement's constructor
$title = new DOMElement('title', 'Mass Effect: Revelation');
$author = new DOMElement('author', 'Drew Karpashin');
$pages = new DOMElement('pages', '336');
$format = new DOMElement('format', 'Mass Market Paperback');

// Using DOMDocument
$publisher = $DOMdoc->createElement('publisher', 'Del Rey');
$year = $DOMdoc->createElement('year', '2007');
$language = $DOMdoc->createElement('language', 'English');
```

As you've probably guessed, DOMDocument's createElement( ) method acts as a factory for DOMElement objects, accepting a tag name, and optionally a value, and returning an instance of the DOMElement class. With that, we can check Step 1 off our list.

Working from the inside out would lead us to create the DOMAttr object at this point. My workflow would prefer that, but we'll see a quirk of attributes below that will explain why I'm deviating from the steps. So let's create the Book element.

```
$MEbook = new DOMElement('book');
```

Notice I didn't pass in a value. We want to leave this element blank to accept child nodes.

We can also create DOMAttr objects with the new operator or via DOMDocument.

```
$ISBN = new DOMAttr('ISBN', '034549816X');
```

or

```
$ISBN = $DOMdoc->createAttribute('ISBN');
```

Why didn't I pass a value in to createAttribute()? That's the rather inconvenient quirk I mentioned above: *createAttribute() doesn't accept a value parameter.* Using this approach, we would have to set DOMAttr's $value property, as demonstrated below, and call DOMElement's setAttributeNode() method to add the $ISBN object to our $MEbook node. If this were the only approach to creating attributes, we could have created it in step 2 as our workflow suggested.

```
$ISBN->value = '034549816X';
```

Another quirk of DOM is that a newly created object isn't modifiable until it has been added to the DOMDocument. So to call setAttributeNode(), we first must add our book node to the DOMDocument object.

```
$DOMdoc->firstChild->appendChild($MEbook);
$MEbook->setAttributeNode($ISBN);
```

I called appendChild() on the firstChild property so it inserts itself inside the <library> tag, which is technically the first node. Creating a DOMAttr object with the new operator is easier but still requires the call to setAttributeNode(). Fortunately, there's a better way. DOMElement defines another method for setting attributes called setAttribute(). With it, we can set our key, value, and add it to the element in one swell foop.

```
$MEbook->setAttribute('ISBN', '034549816X');
$MEbook->setAttribute('id', 'B6');
```

Note that $MEbook must still be added to $DOMdoc before we can call setAttribute(). That finishes steps 1-3, and thanks to setAttribute(), we can skip step 5. But let's not be too hasty. Step 4 is still looming.

Adding children to an element isn't difficult. It's such a common procedure that there are two methods defined in DOMNode to allow us to do so. The simplest is appendChild().

```
$MEbook->appendChild($title);
$MEbook->appendChild($pages);
$MEbook->appendChild($format);
$MEbook->appendChild($publisher);
$MEbook->appendChild($year);
$MEbook->appendChild($language);
```

As the name suggests, `appendChild()` simply adds the child node to the end of the node on which it's called. There's something wrong with our $MEbook node though: we forgot to append the $author element. Fortunately, DOMNode gives us a tool to correct that mistake: the `insertBefore()` method.

```
$MEbook->insertBefore($author, $pages);
```

This call inserts our $author node before the $pages node, right where it should be. If the second parameter is omitted, `insertBefore()` adds the node to the end, just like `appendChild()`.

Because $MEbook was added to our DOMDocument above, which was necessary to make it editable, our work is done. We can see the result with `saveXML()`, which we'll discuss in greater detail shortly.

```
echo $DOMdoc->saveXML();
```

By default, the book we just added will appear with the tags rammed together on a single line. DOMDocument includes a nifty property that should clean that up for us: `formatOutput`. The text still appears on a single line even if we've set `$DOMdoc->formatOutput=true;` To get the output you expect, we must also set `preserveWhiteSpace` to `false` before we load the document. So unless you're building a minified XML document meant to only be machine readable, you'll want to output it in this manner:

```
$DOMdoc = new DOMDocument();
$DOMdoc->preserveWhiteSpace = false;
$DOMdoc->load('library.xml');

// More code here
$DOMdoc->firstChild->appendChild($MEbook);

// Append our $MEbook nodes, as above
$DOMdoc->formatOutput = true;
echo $DOMdoc->saveXML();
```

Editing with DOM

DOM has many more methods defined for modifying XML documents than SimpleXML. We'll go over editing in more detail in *Chapter 6: Advanced DOM*, but I'll give you a taste here.

Like SimpleXML, you can also change values of DOM nodes with variable assignment syntax. You might not have noticed but we misspelled the author's name for *Mass Effect: Revelation* above. Let's correct that:

```
$author->nodeValue = 'Drew Karpyshyn';
```

But what if we are asked to remove all science fiction novels, such as *Halo* and *Mass Effect* from our library? We can do that. Where SimpleXML stops with modifying values of nodes, DOM allows you to move and to alter entire nodes. One such editing method DOM provides will solve our problem nicely: removeChild().

removeChild() expects a DOMNode object to be passed in. We already have our *Mass Effect* title in such an object, so removing it will be simple.

```
$DOMdoc->firstChild->removeChild($MEbook);
```

The *Halo* title is slightly more challenging. Because we haven't studied XPath with DOM yet, we'll have to fall back on that JavaScript-esque method, getElementsByTagName().

```
$NodeList = $DOMdoc->getElementsByTagName('book');
$HaloBook = $NodeList->item(4);
```

The data for these book is still safely stored our $MEbook and $HaloBook variables, ready to append to another DOM object if we wanted to save them.

Returning to XML

Though it might be fun to keep your DOMDocument objects around to trade with your PHP-programming friends, eventually you'll need to output your DOMDocument as XML to share with the world. As with loading XML, DOM provides several methods for accomplishing this task.

First on the roster is the partner to load(): save(). Just as load() inputs a well-formed XML file from disk, save() outputs a well-formed XML file to disk. It accepts a file path parameter and optionally some libxml constants as options.

```
$DOMdoc->save('/var/documents/library.xml');
```

Naturally, there is also a similarly named partner to loadXML(), loadHTML(), and loadHTMLFile(). So to return your DOMDocument as an XML string:

```
echo $DOMdoc->saveXML();
```

saveXML() also accepts a node parameter and libxml constants. As such, if we only wanted our Halo title back as a string, we could pass it in like so:

```
echo $DOMdoc->saveXML($HaloBook);
```

Be warned that passing in a node in this manner will prevent saveXML() from returning the <?xml...?> declaration.

Had we constructed our DOMdocument as XHTML, we could save it to our web server in this manner:

```
$DOMdoc->saveHTMLFile('/var/www/htdocs/library.html');
```

We could also return it as a string, perhaps to save back to a database.

```
$HTMLstring = $DOMdoc->saveHTML();
```

saveHTML() also accepts a DOMNode parameter like saveXML() so you can return HTML snippets rather than the entire document. Unlike the XML handling methods, the HTML methods do not accept libxml parameters.

The Road Ahead

I hope you have a better understanding of how powerful the DOM library is. We've looked at several methods for loading XML and HTML data and how to create new nodes programmatically, and we have had a glimpse of DOM's ability to modify XML. Our ability to parse XML seemed a bit stunted though. We'll overcome that in our next chapter, where XPath will place the entire document at our fingertips.

Chapter
6

Advanced DOM

What This Chapter is Not

This chapter isn't a comprehensive look at every advanced
feature in the DOM library. The DOM library is enormous. We are
going to examine DOM's approach to some advanced XML features.
A more comprehensive reference to the DOM library can be found
in _Appendix B_.

XPath

We've discussed XPath several times, but DOM is where it really becomes essential.

Let's start by loading our library file.

```
$DOMdoc = new DOMDocument();
$DOMdoc->load('library.xml');
```

To perform XPath queries with DOM, we must create an XPath object using a DOMDocument object.

```
$xpath = new DOMXpath($DOMdoc);
```

Remember our query for all book nodes from *Chapter 2*? We can retrieve all book nodes with the absolute XPath expression /library/book. Here's how we put it to work.

```
$myNodeList = $xpath->query('/library/book');
foreach ($myNodeList as $node) {
    echo $node->nodeValue;
}
```

That gets us a DOMNodeList object filled with DOMNodes of each book. We can loop through it and act on each node. Let's say we only care about book titles, and we want to avoid the overhead of looping. We can use a relative query.

```
$titleList = $xpath->query('book/title');
foreach ($titleList as $node) {
    echo $node->nodeValue; //Prints all titles
}
```

Note that we omitted the leading slash and library. Our XPath query read book/title, not /library/book/title to make it a relative path. Because we provided no second parameter, the context node is set to the root node, so the two queries are equivalent, but consider this:

```
$myNodeList = $xpath->query('/library/book');
$contextNode = $myNodeList->item(2);
$title = $xpath->query('title', $contextNode);
echo $title->item(0)->nodeValue;
// prints "Alice's Adventures in Wonderland"
```

This relative query returns the third title because we set the context node to the third book in the list rather than the root. In fact, executing that query in root context would return nothing because "library" has no "title" node. What if we wanted to jump to the next title in the list?

```
echo $title->item(1)->nodeValue;
// prints nothing
```

Whoops! Why did we get an empty string back instead of "A Christmas Carol"? When we pass a context node, as far as XPath is concerned, the rest of the document doesn't exist. Even though our 'title' query returned a DOMNodeList, it had only one member.

Remember we can get to attributes by preceding our node name with the @ sign.

```
$ISBNlist = $xpath->query('/library/book/@ISBN');
```

Because almost everything in an XML document is a node, $ISBNlist is a DOMNodeList that we can loop through just like our $titleList.

Consider this query:

```
$ISBNlist = $xpath->query('/library/book[@ISBN]');
```

That doesn't give us the value of ISBN attributes; rather, it gives us every book node that HAS an ISBN attribute.

XPath Predicates

Let's look at some practical examples of XPath predicates. Recall that they use a syntax very similar to PHP's array notation.

```
$firstBook = $xpath->query('/library/book[1]/title');
echo $firstBook->item(0)->nodeValue; //Prints "Pride and
Prejudice"
```

A predicate is always contained in brackets after a node name. A useful extension to the attribute predicate is looking for a specific attribute.

```
$publicDomainBooks = $xpath->query('book[@ISBN="NA"]');
```

@ISBN="NA" returns only those books with an ISBN attribute of NA. Now let's play with some predicate functions.

```
$lastBook = $xpath->query('book[last()]');
```

Predictably, this returns the last book. We can also perform simple math with the results of these functions.

```
$penultimateBook = $xpath->query('book[last() - 1]');
```

This returns the next-to-last book.

```
$fourthBook = $xpath->query('book[position() = 4]');
```

This returns the fourth book because XPath counts starting at one. Another useful thing we can do with the position() function is:

```
$firstThreeBooks = $xpath->query('book[position() < 4]');
```

We can also search for specific elements contained in a node, not just attributes. Say we wanted all books published after a given year.

```
$recentBooks = $xpath->query('book[year > 1999]');
```

Notice that to access elements rather than attributes, we simply omit the @ inside the brackets. Recall that you can also extend the query past any of these predicates:

```
$threeTitles = $xpath->query('book[position() < 4]/title');
```

XPath Shortcuts

Another way to get at all the titles in the document, besides the relative queries we examined above, is with this shortcut query:

```
$titleList = $xpath->query('book//title');
```

This tells XPath to find all <title> nodes that are descendants of <book> nodes but to ignore titles of all other node types, like hypothetical <video> nodes.

Perhaps we'd like ISBNs with our titles. We can combine XPath queries with the pipe symbol |. The query method returns all matching nodes as a flat DOMNodeList. The order of matching nodes in the XML document affects their order in the result.

```
$titleList = $xpath->query('book/@ISBN | book/title');
foreach ($titleList as $node) {
    echo "{$node->nodeName} = {$node->nodeValue}\n";
}
```

Would output:

```
title = Pride and Prejudice
ISBN = NA
title = The Adventures of Sherlock Holmes
ISBN = NA
title = Alice's Adventures in Wonderland
ISBN = NA
title = A Christmas Carol
ISBN = 0765328321
title = Halo: The Fall of Reach
```

XPath wildcards are the familiar * character. This is how XPath allows a program to self-discover and parse a document when its structure is unknown. There isn't a wildcard to select every node regardless of type; instead, XPath provides a function: node().

```
$myNodeList = $xpath->query('node()');
```

Finally, PHP offers its own XPath shortcut of sorts. Rather than using the query() method as we have throughout these examples, DOM provides an evaluate() method, which not only executes the XPath query, but attempts to return the data as a PHP data type rather than a DOMNodeList. So we could echo our title directly this way:

```
echo $xpath->evaluate('string(book[1]/title)');
```

evaluate() is rather fussy and often returns a DOMNodeList just like query(). Remember that white space is often considered a node unto itself and can confuse parsers. Wrapping our query in XPath's string() function allows PHP to correctly type the result.

XPath Axes

We'll end our discussion of XPath in DOM with a quick example using XPath Axes.

```
$myNodeList = $xpath->query('book');
$firstBook = $myNodeList->item(0);
$allChildren = $xpath->query('child::*', $firstBook);
$allTextDescendants = $xpath->query('descendant::text()',
$firstBook);
```

`child::*` returns all child nodes of the `$firstBook` node by combining the `child::` axes with the * wildcard. Refer back to *Chapter 2* if these examples don't look familiar.

Namespaces in DOM

Parsing with Namespaces

For a review of the definition of namespaces, see *Chapter 1*.

Returning to the MXML example introduced in Chapter 1, let's see how DOM parses the same data. Once again, let's assume we've loaded the Flex document in *Appendix E* into a variable called `$FlexDoc`. Loading the data is identical to the earlier process.

```
$DOMdoc = new DOMDocument();
$DOMdoc->loadXML($FlexDoc);
```

Unlike SimpleXML, which has optional namespace parameters accompanying its method calls, `DOMDocument` defines separate methods for parsing with namespaces. The methods are named nearly identically to the non-namespace versions, with the addition of `NS` at the end. Therefore, to extract elements without a namespace, we can call `getElementsByTagName()`. To extract with a namespace, we call `getElementsByTagNameNS()`. The next difference from SimpleXML is that DOM's namespace parameters come *before* the element's name. To load my `<mx:LineChart>` element, we have to call it in this way:

```
$myDOMNodeList = $DOMdoc->getElementsByTagNameNS(
    'library://ns.adobe.com/flex/mx', 'LineChart'
);
echo $DOMdoc->saveXML($myDOMNodeList->item(0));
```

Notice also that the namespace is specified by its URI, not its prefix. Remember that the saveXML() method must be called on the DOMDocument object, and we pass in the DOMNode object we want returned as a string, in this case $myDOMNodeList->item(0).

Attributes are extracted in a similar manner:

```
$myDOMnode = $myDOMNodeList->item(0);
$myDOMattr = $myDOMnode->getAttributeNodeNS(
    'library://ns.adobe.com/flex/mx', 'dataProvider'
);
```

As we mentioned in *Chapter 1*, attributes rarely have namespaces associated with them directly; the namespace is normally associated with the element. As such, getAttributeNodeNS() isn't especially useful, and you'll use getAttributeNode() more often, even with namespaces. If you run the example above, it won't return anything, as the attributes for <mx:LineChart> are not namespace qualified. To actually get the value of the dataProvider attribute, we'll have to extract it as usual.

```
$myDOMnode = $myDOMNodeList->item(0);
$myDOMattr = $myDOMnode->getAttributeNode('dataProvider');
echo $DOMdoc->saveXML($myDOMattr);
```

Extracting a single node with its ID tag is no different from what we saw in *Chapter 5*. getElementById() doesn't have a corresponding namespace method. When you think about it, this makes sense. You're accessing one specific node by its ID attribute, which must be unique, so the namespace isn't necessary except in the rarest of cases.

Unfortunately, DOM doesn't provide us with a method as convenient as SimpleXML's children() call to parse the entire document. Let's look at an example that will allow us to do that DOM-style. Perhaps surprisingly, DOM offers little support for self-discovering the namespaces in the document. As with SimpleXML, it's necessary to parse each namespace separately. Let's assume we know our namespace prefixes.

Listing 6.1: Parsing with Namespaces

```php
<?php
$namespaces = array('s', 'mx', 'fx');
$xpath = new DOMXpath($DOMdoc);
foreach ($namespaces as $ns) {
    $xpath->registerNamespace(
        $ns, $DOMdoc->lookupNamespaceURI($ns)
    );
}

$myNodeArray = array();
foreach ($namespaces as $ns) {
    $searchString = "//$ns:*";
    $myNodeArray[$ns] = $xpath->query($searchString);
}

foreach ($myNodeArray as $ns => $myNodeList) {
    for ($i=0; $i<$myNodeList->length; $i++) {
        $myNode = $myNodeList->item($i);
        echo $myNode->nodeName . ':' . $myNode->nodeValue;
    }
}
```

A great deal is happening in that little code snippet in Listing 6.1. First, I declare an array of my namespace prefixes. (We could also have extracted them with SimpleXML.)

```php
$namespaces = array('s', 'mx', 'fx');
```

Next, I create a DOMXPath object for parsing. Recall from *Chapter 4* that most of DOM's traversing power comes from XPath rather than PHP functions like SimpleXML's `children()`.

```php
$xpath = new DOMXpath($DOMdoc);
```

I loop through my namespaces and register them with XPath. Registering the namespaces allows me to use the prefixes in XPath queries. This isn't necessary in every case—PHP is a forgiving language after all—but it's a good practice so they'll be available for you every time you need them. Registering a prefix with XPath naturally requires the namespace URI, but we can avoid hard-coding it with the useful `DOMDocument::lookupNamespaceURI()` method.

```php
foreach ($namespaces as $ns) {
    $xpath->registerNamespace(
        $ns, $DOMdoc->lookupNamespaceURI($ns)
    );
}
```

Finally, I'm ready to parse. For this exercise, I've simply collected my nodes into an associative array that groups DOMNodeList objects with their namespace prefix.

```php
$myNodeArray = array();
foreach ($namespaces as $ns) {
    $searchString = "//$ns:*";
    $myNodeArray[$ns] = $xpath->query($searchString);
}
```

I can then loop through the namespaces and then loop again through the DOMNodeList to access each node and print it out.

```php
foreach ($myNodeArray as $ns=>$myNodeList) {
    for ($i=0; $i<$myNodeList->length; $i++) {
        $myNode = $myNodeList->item($i);
        echo $myNode->nodeName . ':' . $myNode->nodeValue;
    }
}
```

Notice the XPath query. // means "find this node wherever it is in the document," followed by the namespace prefix (as a variable), followed by *, which is the wildcard for all nodes. The query is saying "Find every node in this namespace, regardless of where it appears in the document."

```php
$searchString = "//$ns:*";
```

This parsing example should give you the tools to experiment with more complicated parsing tasks.

Creating with Namespaces

The most important principle to remember when creating with DOM is *ADD* before you *ALTER*. Any new object you create must be added to the document before you can modify it, for example, by assigning attributes to a node or changing a value.

Recall from *Chapter 5* that Elements can be created in two ways: via their own constructor or via DOMDocument's `createElement()` method. The constructor works in similar fashion to SimpleXML's methods in that it accepts a namespace URL as its final parameter. Creating with DOMDocument uses similar methods to those we used in Chapter 5 but with NS appended to the end. Regardless of which method we choose, we'll start as we always do: with a new DOMDocument, but we won't load any data this time.

```
$DOMdoc = new DOMDocument('1.0', 'utf-8');
```

Because I'm creating the document from scratch rather than loading an existing XML document, I take the extra step of specifying the XML version and character encoding in the constructor.

```
$rootElement = new DOMElement(
    's:Application',
    null,
    'library://ns.adobe.com/flex/spark');
```

We pass null in as the second parameter, as we don't want to specify a text value for the root node.

```
$rootElement = $DOMdoc->createElementNS(
    'library://ns.adobe.com/flex/spark', 's:Application'
);
```

In contrast to the DOMElement constructor, the DOMDocument method follows the pattern of the DOM methods we've looked at up to this point: a familiar method with NS appended to the end.

To declare a prefix for the namespace, specify the prefix as part of the element name. For example, `new DOMElement('Application', ...)` will honor the namespace but not produce a prefix. `new DOMElement('s:Application', ...)` will honor the namespace and create a prefix of `s:` for that namespace.

Namespaces don't need to be declared explicitly. They are added to the document automatically as you add them via elements and attribute nodes. Speaking of which, let's add our root element to the document.

```
$DOMdoc->appendChild($rootElement);
```

Continuing the construction process:

```
$lineChart = new DOMElement(
    'mx:LineChart',
    null,
    'library://ns.adobe.com/flex/mx'
);
$rootElement->appendChild($lineChart);

$horizAxis = new DOMElement(
    'mx:horizontalAxis',
    null,
    'library://ns.adobe.com/flex/mx'
);
$series = new DOMElement(
    'mx:series',
    null,
    'library://ns.adobe.com/flex/mx'
);
$lineChart->appendChild($horizAxis);
$lineChart->appendChild($series);

echo $DOMdoc->saveXML();
```

Strictly speaking, it is not necessary to include the namespace URL once the namespace has been declared in the document. In the current version of DOM...

```
$horizAxis = new DOMElement(
    'mx:horizontalAxis',
    null,
    'library://ns.adobe.com/flex/mx'
);
```

and

```
$horizAxis = new DOMElement('mx:horizontalAxis');
```

...are functionally equivalent after the namespace has been declared. Future versions may not be as forgiving.

And with that, we have the beginnings of a Flex application.

CDATA

Recall that a A Flex application can rarely stand on MXML alone, since MXML just defines the user interface. In general, there must be some ActionScript to do the processing. Because ActionScript is not an XML-compatible language, it must be contained within a CDATA block.

To add such a block, we'll use DOM's CDATA constructor, exactly like we did in _Chapter 5_. Let's assume we've loaded some valid ActionScript code into a variable called $ActionScript.

```
$ActionScriptCDATA = new DOMCdataSection($ActionScript);
$ActionScriptNode = new DOMElement(
    'fx:Script',
    null,
    'http://ns.adobe.com/mxml/2009'
);
$DOMdoc->appendChild($ActionScriptNode);
$ActionScriptNode->appendChild($ActionScriptCDATA);
```

Comments

DOM also provides a class for adding comment nodes to the document. Because XML is meant to be human readable, you can use them to document your document.

```
$comment = new DOMComment('This is a comment');
$DOMdoc->appendChild($comment);
```

Moving Data

SimpleXML doesn't provide facilities for moving data. While DOM does, it isn't as obvious as you might think. insertBefore() is the magic function that will do the heavy lifting for us. First, we need to extract the node we want to move and then call insertBefore() on the node that we want to follow it. Let's return to our library example for simplicity.

```
$DOMdoc = new DOMDocument();
$DOMdoc->formatOutput = true;
$DOMdoc->load('library.xml');

$xpath = new DOMXPath($DOMdoc);
$nodeList = $xpath->query('//book');

$book2move = $nodeList->item(3);
$book = $nodeList->item(2);
$book2move->insertBefore($book);
```

Naturally if we wanted to move an element to the end, we could simply call appendChild() once we'd extracted the node. Both insertBefore() and appendChild() move elements by default. It is necessary to call cloneNode() on the extracted node before calling either of those functions to create a copy of a node.

Removing Data

SimpleXML also provides no facility for deleting nodes. DOM gives us that ability via three methods: removeChild() for elements, removeAttribute() for attributes, and the less intuitively named deleteData() for CDATA. Let's assume we have our node list from above.

```
$book2remove = $nodeList->item(3);
$book2remove->parentNode->removeChild($book2remove);
```

Notice we need to call it against the parent node. The easiest way is to simply use the parentNode attribute of the node we are removing.

Normalizing

"Normalizing" an XML document puts the document into "normal" form. Just what is normal form?

The key point to remember about normalizing is that its primary effect is on text nodes. If you've ever attempted to parse an HTML document with pure JavaScript (not a framework like jQuery or YUI), you'll have some idea how meddlesome text nodes can be. In some cases, DOM treats whitespace between tags as a node unto itself, such that

```
<p></p>
This is a text node.
```

has a different DOM structure than does

```
<p></p>
This is
a text node.
```

The line break separating "This is" from "a text node." in the second example is considered an empty text node and therefore part of the document structure. Obviously, this is a bad example. We probably want our text nodes inside the <p> tags, but for illustration, let's assume we haven't caught that mistake yet.

Normalizing the document cleans up the text nodes by removing blank nodes and ensuring that no two text nodes are side by side, among other things, which makes the document easier to parse and keeps extensions like XPointer from breaking. This should have the same effect as does closing and reloading the DOM document.

Let's see what happens to our example above before and after normalization in Listing 6.2.

Listing 6.2: After Normalization

```php
<?php
$DOMdoc = new DOMDocument();
$DOMdoc->formatOutput = true;

// create a note element
$note = new DOMElement('note', 'Plan code review. ');
$due = new DomText("Due next week. ");
$priority = new DomText("High priority. ");

// add note to our document
$DOMdoc->appendChild($note);

// add text to note element
$note->appendChild($due);
$note->appendChild($priority);

echo "Before: " . $note->childNodes->length . "\n";
$note->normalize();
echo "After:  " . $note->childNodes->length . "\n";
echo $DOMdoc->saveXML();
```

Outputs the following:

```
Before: 3
After:  1
<?xml version="1.0"?>
<note>Plan code review. Due next week. High priority.</note>
```

Officially, normalization:

Puts all Text nodes in the full depth of the sub-tree underneath this Node, including attribute nodes, into a 'normal' form where only structure (e.g., elements, comments, processing instructions, CDATA sections, and entity references) separates Text nodes, i.e., there are neither adjacent Text nodes nor empty Text nodes. This can be used to ensure that the DOM view of a document is the same as if it were saved and reloaded and is useful when operations (such as XPointer lookups) that depend on a particular document tree structure are to be used.[1]

[1] http://www.w3.org/TR/DOM-Level-2-Core/core.html

Loading from SimpleXML

Converting a DOM object to SimpleXML is as simple as converting the other way. To recap *Chapter 4*, both SimpleXML and DOM provide a function that converts an object to one of the other type. In the case of DOM, this is the *only* non-Object-Oriented function defined. To convert your DOM object to SimpleXML, the call is:

```
$SimpleXMLElementObj = simplexml_import_dom($mxml);
```

This allows you to make use of SimpleXML's simplicity.

The Road Ahead

Though we've spent the last several pages examining advanced techniques with DOM, there is much more power hiding in the library. You now have the tools to investigate further.

Chapter 7

Basic XMLReader & XMLWriter

How It Compares

XMLReader is PHP's implementation of an XML pull parser.

You may have heard of SAX—the Simple API for XML. PHP 4's DOMXML bears many characteristics of a SAX implementation: parsing the document as a stream, handling each tag as a callback, and complete lack of awareness about what happens before or after the cursor's location in the file. We have already discussed the disadvantages of DOMXML in *Chapter 1*.

SimpleXML and DOM both approach XML parsing from a DOM-based perspective. In other words, they create a representation of the entire document in memory. This makes it easy to jump to random locations in the file and move nodes around but takes a toll on system resources.

StAX is an attempt to split the difference between these two approaches. StAX stands for "Streaming API for XML" (*http://en.wikipedia.org/wiki/StAX*). It approaches XML parsing similar to some database access libraries: by implementing a cursor that points to a specific location in the file.

With StAX, programmers can move the cursor around in the file and do a simple test to see whether we've found the data we want before reading an entire node. StAX has the advantage—and disadvantage—of knowing the complete contents of the node it is pointing to. For small nodes, this makes it memory efficient while still offering an object representation of the node for easy manipulation. For large nodes, like the root node, for example, StAX has all the disadvantages of SimpleXML or DOM. Parse with caution!

XMLReader Workflow

We'll start by opening an XML document, either by file path or by URL.

Note that there are a number of gotchas in XMLReader that you won't find in SimpleXML and DOM. Unlike both of those libraries, simply opening the document doesn't read it into memory. Rather, XMLReader won't read a thing until you tell it to.

While using XMLReader requires a couple of extra steps, you gain memory savings. Instead of creating a RAM-crushing representation of an entire document in memory, it reads in bite-size chunks. How big are those chunks? That's largely up to you.

XMLReader reads by node. Because essentially everything in XML is a node, you can walk through a document in a dainty, memory-preserving manner to the nodes you want and read only those. This, however, means you have to navigate some of the perils of an XML tree from which SimpleXML and DOM protect you.

Before I make you too paranoid, let's look at a simple example of reading our library and dumping it to the screen.

```
$XMLreaderDoc = new XMLReader();
$XMLreaderDoc->open('library.xml');
$XMLreaderDoc->read();
echo $XMLreaderDoc->readOuterXML();
$XMLreaderDoc->close();
```

This spits out our entire document. Wait a minute! Didn't we just say XMLReader's advantage is that it doesn't read the entire document into memory? Why did it echo the entire document?

Remember that we also said XMLReader reads by node, and the very first node in any XML document is the root node, which contains all other nodes in the document. Therefore, if you just open a document and immediately readOuterXML(), you've effectively defeated the primary reason for using XMLReader. This is the first caution I mentioned in the introduction.

Before we solve that problem, the read() and readOuterXML() statements need some explanation. The first read() method is what actually instructs XMLReader to move the cursor to a node. It doesn't actually read much, other than its position. The read<Something>() methods do the work of returning the data as a string in various permutations.

Now, let's adjust our example above and see whether we can get just one <book> node.

```
$XMLreaderDoc = new XMLReader();
$XMLreaderDoc->open('library.xml');
$XMLreaderDoc->next(); //Moves the cursor to <library>
$XMLreaderDoc->read(); //Moves the cursor to the next node
echo $XMLreaderDoc->readOuterXML(); //Actually reads data
$XMLreaderDoc->close();
```

But if you run this you'll notice that it does not output anything, what happened?

This is another of those XML pitfalls that DOM and SimpleXML guard against. Because our library.xml data is formatted for human readability with whitespace, we actually just moved the cursor past the <library> node to the text node that contains nothing but whitespace. So it did print; there just wasn't anything to print. It looks something like this.

Step 1:

```
$XMLreaderDoc->open('library.xml'); //No cursor
```

Step 2:

```
$XMLreaderDoc->next();
CURSOR-><library>
    <book>
    . . .
//No data in memory
```

Step 3:

```
$XMLreaderDoc->read(); //Move cursor
<library>CURSOR->(empty text node)
    <book>
    . . .
//whitespace in memory
```

We can finally get to our data with one more call to read().

Step 4:

```
$XMLreaderDoc->read(); //Move cursor
<library>
CURSOR-><book>
    . . .
//<book> node in memory
```

The code looks like this:

```
$XMLreaderDoc = new XMLReader();
$XMLreaderDoc->open('library.xml');
$XMLreaderDoc->next(); //Moves the cursor to <library>
$XMLreaderDoc->read(); //Moves the cursor to empty text
$XMLreaderDoc->read(); //Moves the cursor to <book>
echo $XMLreaderDoc->readOuterXML(); //Returns data
$XMLreaderDoc->close();
```

That's better. At least we obtained our data, but that example likely raises all sorts of questions of the "there has to be a better way" variety. Before I address those, let's discuss the difference between read() and next(). You may be wondering why we didn't do a call to next() in place of our first read(). There is a crucial difference between the two: read() moves from from node to node in order, without skipping anything. next(), however, moves between siblings, skipping all child nodes. Watch what happens when we call next() twice.

```
$XMLreaderDoc->next();
CURSOR->library>
    <book>
    . . .

$XMLreaderDoc->next();
    . . .
    </book>
</library>
CURSOR->
```

The second next() call skipped all child nodes, in other words, all the <book> nodes, and went right to the end of the document looking for another <library> node!

read(), on the other hand, skips nothing whatsoever, including blank text nodes. In most cases, we don't want those. We can skip them by brute force as in Listing 7.1.

Listing 7.1 Skipping blank nodes.

```php
<?php
$XMLreaderDoc = new XMLReader();
$XMLreaderDoc->open('library.xml');
$XMLreaderDoc->next(); //Moves the cursor to <library>
$XMLreaderDoc->read(); //Moves the cursor to empty text
if ($XMLreaderDoc->name == '#text') {
    //If text node, move on
    $XMLreaderDoc->read(); //Moves the cursor to <book>
}
echo $XMLreaderDoc->readOuterXML(); //Returns data
$XMLreaderDoc->close();
```

Here we used the name property of the XMLReader object to check at which node the cursor was pointing. We can dodge our blank text nodes that way, but it probably won't take much imagination to realize that constant tests for blank nodes will make the task of parsing a processor-hogging minefield. This is where the LIBXML constants come to the rescue. We can pass some Libxml constants to the open() method to strip out all those obnoxious text nodes. For the full list of Libxml constants, see *Appendix F*.

Back to Libxml constants. Probably the most useful one is LIBXML_NOBLANKS. As the name suggests, it removes blank text nodes. A couple of other handy constants are LIBXML_COMPACT, which can speed up parsing, and LIBXML_PARSEHUGE, which removes size limitations from the parser. For space, we'll just use LIBXML_NOBLANKS starting in Listing 7.2.

Listing 7.2 Using LIBXML_NOBLANKS constant.

```php
<?php
$XMLreaderDoc = new XMLReader();
$XMLreaderDoc->open(
    'library.xml', 'utf-8', LIBXML_NOBLANKS
);

//Moves the cursor to <library>
$XMLreaderDoc->next();

//No empty text node, so cursor at <book>
$XMLreaderDoc->read();

echo $XMLreaderDoc->readOuterXML();

$XMLreaderDoc->close();
```

Let's say we only want titles. Let's extend our example to get those for us in Listing 7.3.

Listing 7.3 Reading titles with XMLReader

```php
<?php
$XMLreaderDoc = new XMLReader();
$XMLreaderDoc->open(
    'library.xml', 'utf-8', LIBXML_NOBLANKS
);

$XMLreaderDoc->next();

while ($XMLreaderDoc->read()) {
    if ($XMLreaderDoc->name == 'title')
        echo $XMLreaderDoc->readInnerXML()."\n";
}

$XMLreaderDoc->close();
```

Here we open the file with LIBXML_NOBLANKS to remove the stray text nodes, call next() to move the cursor to the root node, and then loop through every node, testing the name property until we find <title> nodes. Once we've found the node we want, we echo the contents of the node with a call to readInnerXML().

There's another enigma about read() that might be bothering you a bit. We said read() touches every node, and essentially everything in XML is a node. In our discussion of DOM, we also said that even attributes are considered nodes, but read() didn't take us to any attributes, did it? It's true that read() skips attributes, but that doesn't mean we can't get to them. In fact, XMLReader provides a number of methods to access attributes, both by name and, perhaps unexpectedly, by number.

Let's print out titles with their ISBN number, as in Listing 7.4.

Listing 7.4 Echo titles and ISBNs with XMLReader

```php
<?php
$XMLreaderDoc = new XMLReader();
$XMLreaderDoc->open(
    'library.xml', 'utf-8', LIBXML_NOBLANKS
);

$XMLreaderDoc->next();
while ($XMLreaderDoc->read()) {
    if ($XMLreaderDoc->name == 'book') {
        $ISBN = $XMLreaderDoc->getAttribute('ISBN');
    }
    if ($XMLreaderDoc->name == 'title') {
        echo "$ISBN : " . $XMLreaderDoc->readInnerXML()
            . "\n";
    }
}

$XMLreaderDoc->close();
```

We could have also called $XMLreaderDoc->getAttributeNo(1); to return the ISBN number, but I prefer using names. Still, it helps to know the method is available when you're parsing an unknown document.

There is something you may have noticed in our example above and that's even more obvious with this example: we're getting blank titles in between each printed line. Why is that?

If we were to call `readOuterXML()` on those title nodes, we'd see two `<title>` nodes for each book, one that looks like:

```
<title>The Adventures of Sherlock Holmes</title>
```

and one that looks like `<title/>`. That is, the name property returns "title" for both the opening and closing tags. As such, we can eliminate those extra lines by changing the `if` statement above to:

```
if ($XMLreaderDoc->name == 'title'
    && $XMLreaderDoc->readOuterXML() != '<title/>')
```

There is more to XMLReader, but this should get you started.

XMLWriter Workflow

XMLReader has one glaring limitation: it only reads. Fortunately, it has a companion library called XMLWriter that fills the gap.

Supposed that we'd like to use XMLWriter to add a book node to our library similar to the exercise we did in *Chapter 6*. Unfortunately, we can't do that directly.

Just as XMLReader only reads, XMLWriter only writes. That means you can't read a preexisting document into XMLWriter and edit it. Also like XMLReader, XMLWriter has no awareness of the document's structure other than the node on which it's currently working. A notable exception to this rule is that XMLWriter is also aware of the parents to the current working node, meaning it's always aware of the root node, but beyond that, it streams data to its output location in a rather unintelligent but memory-efficient manner.

XMLWriter's methods generally come in two flavors. The simplest takes the form of `writeSomething(<name>, <content>);`. This makes outputting simple text nodes quick and efficient, but you can probably guess it will give us problems with more complex nodes that contain attributes, children, or both. For those, XMLWriter includes companion methods that take the form of `startSomething(<name>);` and `endSomething(<name>);`.

Another quirk of XMLWriter bears mentioning. We just said that XMLWriter streams data to *its output location*. This means we need to declare the output location before streaming. We can't construct a document and then echo the results wherever we want, like we can with SimpleXML and DOM. (Actually, this is possible in a limited way, which we'll see below, but it's not an approach typical of XMLWriter's philosophy.)

Let's construct a simple, one-book library to dip our toes into XMLWriter.

```
$XMLwriterDoc = new XMLWriter();
$XMLwriterDoc->openURI('library.xml');
$XMLwriterDoc->startDocument('1.0','utf-8');
```

We start by creating an XMLWriter object. Next, in the critical difference we just mentioned, we open an output source with a call to openURI(). As the name suggests, this can be a file, a URI on the internet, or any of PHP's built-in data streams. For example, if we wanted to print the results to screen, we'd call openURI() and pass stdout, like so:

```
$XMLwriterDoc->openURI('php://stdout');
```

The URI php://stdout tells PHP to stream to stdout, which is the screen by default.

Finally, we finish setting up our document with a call to startDocument(). Both the version and character set parameters are optional but are recommended.

XMLWriter is unique among the libraries we've examined in that all its object-oriented methods also have procedural equivalents. Setting up the same document procedurally looks like this:

```
$xml_w = xmlwriter_open_uri('php://stdout');
xmlwriter_start_document($xml_w, '1.0', 'utf-8');
```

For almost all the XMLWriter procedure calls, we have to pass the XMLWriter resource as the first parameter. We'll continue with the object-oriented approach through the rest of this chapter, but the final listing will display both approaches.

By default, XMLWriter produces "minified" XML. If we want to add white space to make it more human readable, we need to reset a couple of defaults before we start streaming content.

```
$XMLwriterDoc->setIndent(true);
```

setIndent(true) tells XMLWriter to add line breaks and indents to its output. The default indent is two spaces. I prefer tabs, so let's reset the indent character, too.

```
$XMLwriterDoc->setIndentString("\t");
```

Finally, we can start outputting our document. We don't want the root tag, <library> to automatically close on us, so we'll use a startElement() call rather than writeElement().

```
$XMLwriterDoc->startElement('library');
$XMLwriterDoc->startElement('book');
$XMLwriterDoc->writeAttribute('ISBN','978-0764229275');
```

Our first startElement() call created the opening <library> tag. At this point, we're still working within the opening library tag, as if we'd written <library. We haven't told XMLWriter whether we're going to set any attributes for it. Fortunately, XMLWriter is smart enough to close the tag, effectively outputting a >, when it sees any of several other calls, including startElement(), writeElement(), and text(). If you ever need to force XMLWriter to output a closing >—a call to text('')—that is, text() with an empty string—will do the job. In most cases, though, XMLWriter will do the right thing.

We used the shorter form for the ISBN attribute, as it didn't need to contain anything except text. We could have accomplished the same thing with calls to the more verbose startAttribute() and endAttribute(), but let's finish out our mini-library with writeElement().

```
$XMLwriterDoc->writeElement('title', 'Firebird: A Trilogy');
$XMLwriterDoc->writeElement('author', 'Tyers, Kathy');
$XMLwriterDoc->writeElement('pages', '800');
$XMLwriterDoc->writeElement('format', 'Paperback');
$XMLwriterDoc->writeElement('publisher', 'Bethany House');
$XMLwriterDoc->writeElement('year', '2004');
$XMLwriterDoc->writeElement('language', 'English');
$XMLwriterDoc->endElement();//End book
$XMLwriterDoc->endElement(); //End library

$XMLwriterDoc->endDocument();
```

You can see how we output the </book> and </library> elements with calls to endElement(). XMLWriter keeps track of its current node, so there's no need to specify which tag we're closing. Finally, we call endDocument() to tell XMLWriter that we're done, and it can clean up after itself.

The entire document, in object-oriented style, looks like Listing 7.5.

Listing 7.5 Object-oriented XML Writer

```php
<?php
$XMLwriterDoc = new XMLWriter();
$XMLwriterDoc->openURI('library.xml');
$XMLwriterDoc->startDocument('1.0', 'utf-8');
$XMLwriterDoc->startElement('library');
$XMLwriterDoc->startElement('book');
$XMLwriterDoc->writeAttribute('ISBN', '978-0764229275');

$XMLwriterDoc->writeElement('title', 'Firebird: A Trilogy');

$XMLwriterDoc->writeElement('author', 'Tyers, Kathy');
$XMLwriterDoc->writeElement('pages', '800');
$XMLwriterDoc->writeElement('format', 'Paperback');
$XMLwriterDoc->writeElement('publisher', 'Bethany House');

$XMLwriterDoc->writeElement('year', '2004');
$XMLwriterDoc->writeElement('language', 'English');

$XMLwriterDoc->endElement(); //End book
$XMLwriterDoc->endElement(); //End library

$XMLwriterDoc->endDocument();
```

And procedural style looks like Listing 7.6.

Listing 7.6 Procedural XML Writer

```php
<?php
$xml_w = xmlwriter_open_uri('library.xml');
xmlwriter_start_document($xml_w, '1.0', 'utf-8');
xmlwriter_set_indent($xml_w, true);
xmlwriter_set_indent_string($xml_w, "\t");
xmlwriter_start_element($xml_w, 'library');
xmlwriter_start_element($xml_w, 'book');
xmlwriter_write_attribute($xml_w, 'ISBN', '978-0764229275');
xmlwriter_write_element(
    $xml_w, 'title', 'Firebird: A Trilogy'
);
xmlwriter_write_element($xml_w, 'author', 'Tyers, Kathy');
xmlwriter_write_element($xml_w,'pages','800');
xmlwriter_write_element($xml_w,'format','Paperback');
xmlwriter_write_element($xml_w,'publisher','Bethany House');
xmlwriter_write_element($xml_w,'year','2004');
xmlwriter_write_element($xml_w,'language','English');
xmlwriter_end_element($xml_w);//End book
xmlwriter_end_element($xml_w); //End library
xmlwriter_end_document($xml_w);
```

Before we move on, for the sake of completeness, let's do everything with text() to set values, see Listing 7.7.

Listing 7.7 Using text()

```php
<?php
$XMLwriterDoc = new XMLWriter();
$XMLwriterDoc->openMemory();
$XMLwriterDoc->startDocument('1.0', 'utf-8');

$XMLwriterDoc->setIndent(true);
$XMLwriterDoc->setIndentString("\t");

$XMLwriterDoc->startElement('library');
$XMLwriterDoc->startElement('book');
$XMLwriterDoc->startAttribute('ISBN');
$XMLwriterDoc->text('978-0764229275');
$XMLwriterDoc->endAttribute();

$XMLwriterDoc->startElement('title');
$XMLwriterDoc->text('Firebird: A Trilogy');
$XMLwriterDoc->endElement(); //End title
$XMLwriterDoc->startElement('author');
$XMLwriterDoc->text('Tyers, Kathy');
$XMLwriterDoc->endElement(); //End author
$XMLwriterDoc->startElement('pages');
$XMLwriterDoc->text('800');
$XMLwriterDoc->endElement(); //End pages
$XMLwriterDoc->startElement('format');
$XMLwriterDoc->text('Paperback');
$XMLwriterDoc->endElement(); //End format
$XMLwriterDoc->startElement('publisher');
$XMLwriterDoc->text('Bethany House');
$XMLwriterDoc->endElement(); //End publisher
$XMLwriterDoc->startElement('year');
$XMLwriterDoc->text('2004');
$XMLwriterDoc->endElement(); //End year
$XMLwriterDoc->startElement('language');
$XMLwriterDoc->text('English');
$XMLwriterDoc->endElement(); //End language
$XMLwriterDoc->endElement();//End book

$XMLwriterDoc->endElement(); //End library

$XMLwriterDoc->endDocument();

echo $XMLwriterDoc->outputMemory();
```

Here we didn't use one single `write...()` method. As you can see, this approach will work just fine, though it requires multiple calls to `text()` to place content in your elements and `endElement()` to output closing tags. You'll probably want to stick with our first example unless you specifically need `start...()` calls to add attributes or children.

Notice also that instead of calling `openURI()`, I called `openMemory()` to start the document. This is the approach that contradicts XMLWriter's philosophy I mentioned at the beginning of the section. As the name suggests, `openMemory()` constructs your entire XML document in memory and returns the entire document as a string with a call to `outputMemory()`, which can then be echoed, written to disk, or manipulated in another manner. This defeats the purpose of preserving memory by streaming data directly to disk or network but can prove useful if you're streaming to a remote server and find yourself in a situation with poor connectivity.

The Road Ahead

XMLReader's and XMLWriter's provide a different approach to managing your XML documents. There's more to come, in the next chapter, we'll dive even deeper into the features of these to two libraries. Then we'll finally get to see PHP work with XML in the real world.

Chapter 8

Advanced XMLReader and XMLWriter

Namespaces in XMLReader

XMLReader does include support for namespaces. Similar to DOM, XMLReader provides separate methods to handle namespaces, which are named after the simpler, non-namespace accepting methods with "Ns" tacked on the end. Perhaps surprisingly, there aren't many of them. Many methods, like `next()` and `readOuterXML()`, don't care whether you're working with namespaces or not. They operate on whichever node the cursor is pointing to, regardless of the presence or absence of a namespace identifier.

Because XMLReader's cursor doesn't care whether the node it's pointing to has a namespace or not, almost all the methods that operate on namespaces are related to attributes. The one exception, and probably the most useful of XMLReader's namespace methods, is lookupNamespace(). It operates exactly like DOM's lookupNamespaceURI()—that is, it accepts a prefix and returns the URI associated with that prefix.

Let us again assume that we have loaded the Adobe Flex document in *Appendix E* into a variable called $FlexDoc.

```
$XMLreaderDoc = new XMLReader();
$XMLreaderDoc->xml($FlexDoc, 'utf-8', LIBXML_NOBLANKS);
$XMLreaderDoc->read();
$XMLreaderDoc->read();
echo $XMLreaderDoc->lookupNamespace('mx');
//prints library://ns.adobe.com/flex/mx
```

I call read twice to ensure the root node, which declares the namespaces, has been read. Once the cursor is aware of the namespaces, we can work with the prefixes.

As we've mentioned before, it is more common to assign namespaces to elements rather than attributes. We actually don't have an example of a namespaced attribute in the Flex document, but let's assume we have an attribute of mx:categoryField in our <CategoryAxis> element.

I intentionally left the mx: prefix off <CategoryAxis>. If an attribute shares the same namespace as that of its parent element, the attribute's namespace is effectively ignored. So we're actually working with a hypothetical tag that looks like this:

```
<CategoryAxis mx:categoryField="Month" />
```

Here's how we can parse the value of that attribute:

```
while ($XMLreaderDoc->read()) {
    if ($XMLreaderDoc->localName == 'CategoryAxis') {
        echo $XMLreaderDoc->getAttributeNs(
            'categoryField',
            'library://ns.adobe.com/flex/mx'
        );
        break;
    }
}
```

There's a potential gotcha in that code snippet. My if statement is testing against the localName property instead of name. localName returns the node's name without a namespace prefix. If there were both an <s:CategoryAxis /> element and an <mx:CategoryAxis /> element, and we needed to parse both, localName would be a handy tool to have in our bag. However, in this case, we want the non-namespaced element so we can parse out the namespaced attribute. If there were a <mx:CategoryAxis /> element before our non-namespaced element, this code snippet would attempt to parse mx:categoryField and not find it, as the namespace is assigned to the element. To make the code safer for this case, let's try this:

```
while ($XMLreaderDoc->read()) {
    if ($XMLreaderDoc->name == 'CategoryAxis') {
        echo $XMLreaderDoc->getAttributeNs(
            'categoryField',
            $XMLreaderDoc->lookupNamespace('mx')
        );
        break;
    }
}
```

Similar to a call to getAttributeNs(), we can move the cursor to an attribute node without actually reading it by using moveToAttributeNs(). You probably also noticed that I took advantage of the lookupNamespace() method. I don't make a habit of memorizing namespace URIs, so that provides a simple shortcut to passing the URI by hand. Now that the cursor is pointing at an attribute, we can do some tests on the attribute node.

```
while ($XMLreaderDoc->read()) {
    if ($XMLreaderDoc->name == 'CategoryAxis') {
        $XMLreaderDoc->moveToAttributeNs(
            'categoryField',
            $XMLreaderDoc->lookupNamespace('mx')
        );
        if ($XMLreaderDoc->hasValue) {
            echo "\n$XMLreaderDoc->name is populated";
        }
        break;
    }
}
```

While we're talking about attributes, one more method merits mentioning. It's not specifically a namespace method, but moveToElement() helps any time we're mucking about with attributes. It backs the cursor out to point at the current attribute's parent element. If you were working with one of those XML documents in which every element has multiple attributes, this is an important method to know.

```
while ($XMLreaderDoc->read()) {
    if ($XMLreaderDoc->name == 'CategoryAxis') {
        $XMLreaderDoc->moveToAttributeNs(
            'categoryField',
            $XMLreaderDoc->lookupNamespace('mx')
        );
        if ($XMLreaderDoc->hasValue) {
            echo "\n$XMLreaderDoc->name is populated";
        }
        $XMLreaderDoc->moveToElement();
        echo $XMLreaderDoc->name; //prints CategoryAxis
        break;
    }
}
```

Parser Properties

Parser properties in XMLReader give you a measure of control over how the parser will act as it streams XML data. There are only four, which are listed in *Appendix C*, and three of them revolve around how a DTD will be processed. The tricky part to working with parser properties is timing: setParserProperty() must be called after open() or xml(), but before the first read() or next().

Let's say we're confident the data we're streaming is perfectly valid because this is a trusted XML file that we created ourselves. Because there's no point in wasting time validating perfect data, we want XMLReader to skip the validation step. We can do it perfectly in this manner:

```
$XMLreaderDoc = new XMLReader();
$XMLreaderDoc->xml($FlexDoc, 'utf-8', LIBXML_NOBLANKS);
$XMLreaderDoc->setParserProperty(XMLReader::LOADDTD, true);
while ($XMLreaderDoc->read()) {
    ...
```

The LOADDTD option will load a DTD if it exists but won't use the DTD to validate the data. If someone is deluded enough to challenge our perfection, we can prove him or her wrong by setting the same option to false, thereby validating the data.

```
$XMLreaderDoc->setParserProperty(XMLReader::LOADDTD, false);
```

XMLReader to DOM

What do you do if you have a huge XML document and a memory-strapped server, however you need features that don't exist in XMLReader?

XMLReader provides us a handy method that will convert the current node to a DOM object and thereby leverage all of DOM's functionality while only sipping the memory necessary to represent one node in memory. Once it's in DOM, we can also convert it to SimpleXML if needed. The method is named expand(). Working once again with our $FlexDoc:

```
while ($XMLreaderDoc->read()) {
    if ($XMLreaderDoc->name == 'mx:horizontalAxis') {
        $myDOMnode = $XMLreaderDoc->expand();
        break;
    }
}
echo $myDOMnode->tagName;
```

Why did I call $myDOMnode->tagName, instead of, say saveXML()? expand() returns the node as a DOMElement object, and saveXML() is defined in the DOMDocument class. You can manipulate the node with any of DOMElement's or DOMNode's methods, but to gain the full functionality of DOM, you'll need to add the node to a DOMDocument with a method like importNode().

Namespaces in XMLWriter

Similar to how XMLReader and DOM worked, we will have a set of functions that operate on namespaces that mirror existing ones. In the case of XMLWriter they all end with NS being added to the name.

> *The online documentation for XMLReader uses Ns while XMLWriter uses NS. Since in PHP method and function identifiers are not case-sensitive, it doesn't matter in practice which you use.*

Let's again play with the CategoryAxis element in our $FlexDoc. Because namespaces are usually associated with elements, we'll focus on the element methods, although attribute methods work in a similar fashion. We can create the CategoryAxis element in this manner, as in Listing 8.1.

Listing 8.1: Working with Namespaces

```php
$XMLwriterDoc = new XMLWriter();
$XMLwriterDoc->openURI('php://stdout');
$XMLwriterDoc->startDocument('1.0','utf-8');

$XMLwriterDoc->setIndent(true);
$XMLwriterDoc->setIndentString("\t");

$XMLwriterDoc->startElementNS(
    's',
    'Application',
    'library://ns.adobe.com/flex/spark'
);

    $XMLwriterDoc->startElementNs(
        'mx',
        'CategoryAxis',
        'library://ns.adobe.com/flex/mx'
    );

        $XMLwriterDoc->writeAttribute('categoryField', 'Month');
    $XMLwriterDoc->endElement();

$XMLwriterDoc->endElement();

$XMLwriterDoc->endDocument();
```

If you're comparing the output of this code to the listing in *Appendix E*, you'll notice it is missing something. Our <s:Application> tag only has one namespace defined—the namespace applied to the application tag itself. The mx namespace isn't defined until CategoryAxis is created. In Appendix E, all three namespaces are defined in the root <s:Application> tag. For the namespaces to be available to the entire document, we really want all of them defined in the root element tag. How do we accomplish that?

Your first impulse might be to add them to the second parameter of
`startElementNS()`:

```
$XMLwriterDoc->startElementNS(
    's',
    'Application xmlns:fx="http://ns.adobe.com/mxml/2009"
        xmlns:mx="library://ns.adobe.com/flex/mx"',
    'library://ns.adobe.com/flex/spark'
);
```

However, XMLWriter will not work if you do that. There are a couple of ways
we can accomplish that. One is to use the `writeRaw()` method, which we'll
discuss below, but if you look at the namespace declarations, they look a great
deal like attributes. It turns out we can add them with `writeAttribute()`, see
Listing 8.2.

Listing 8.2: Using `writeAttribute`

```
$XMLwriterDoc->startElementNS(
    's', 'Application', 'library://ns.adobe.com/flex/spark'
);

$XMLwriterDoc->writeAttribute(
    'xmlns:fx', 'http://ns.adobe.com/mxml/2009'
);

$XMLwriterDoc->writeAttribute(
    'xmlns:mx', 'library://ns.adobe.com/flex/mx'
);
$XMLwriterDoc->startElementNs(
    'mx', 'CategoryAxis', 'library://ns.adobe.com/flex/mx'
);
```

The output of this code snippet actually outputs the namespace URI twice:
once in the root element and once in the CategoryAxis element. Calling a
`...NS()` method will always add the namespace URI to the element on which
it's called. If you only want the prefix, we can accomplish that with a call
to plain old `startElement()`. So our completed example (of an incomplete
document) looks like Listing 8.3.

Listing 8.3 Using `startElemement`

```
$XMLwriterDoc = new XMLWriter();
$XMLwriterDoc->openURI('php://stdout');
$XMLwriterDoc->startDocument('1.0','utf-8');

$XMLwriterDoc->setIndent(true);
$XMLwriterDoc->setIndentString("\t");

$XMLwriterDoc->startElementNS(
    's', 'Application', 'library://ns.adobe.com/flex/spark'
);

$XMLwriterDoc->writeAttribute(
    'xmlns:fx', 'http://ns.adobe.com/mxml/2009'
);
$XMLwriterDoc->writeAttribute(
    'xmlns:mx', 'library://ns.adobe.com/flex/mx'
);
$XMLwriterDoc->startElement('mx:CategoryAxis');
$XMLwriterDoc->writeAttribute('categoryField','Month');
$XMLwriterDoc->endElement();
$XMLwriterDoc->endElement();

$XMLwriterDoc->endDocument();
```

CDATA and Comments

XMLWriter includes support for other XML features you need, like CDATA nodes, and even some you may not, like comment sections. Both CData and comment sections have `start...()` and `write...()` methods like elements and attributes.

Let's return to our `library.xml` example, write the Sherlock Holmes CDATA section, and add a comment to it, see Listing 8.4.

Listing 8.4 `library.xml` example with XMLWriter

```php
$XMLwriterDoc = new XMLWriter();
$XMLwriterDoc->openURI('php://stdout');
$XMLwriterDoc->startDocument('1.0','utf-8');

$XMLwriterDoc->setIndent(true);
$XMLwriterDoc->setIndentString("\t");

$XMLwriterDoc->startElement('book');
$XMLwriterDoc->writeAttribute('ISBN', 'NA');

$XMLwriterDoc->writeElement(
    'title', 'The Adventures of Sherlock Holmes'
);
$XMLwriterDoc->writeElement(
    'author', 'Arthur Conan Doyle'
);
$XMLwriterDoc->writeElement('pages', '307');
$XMLwriterDoc->writeElement('format', 'Hardback');
$XMLwriterDoc->writeElement(
    'publisher','George Newnes'
);
$XMLwriterDoc->writeElement('year', '1892');
$XMLwriterDoc->writeElement('language', 'English');
$XMLwriterDoc->writeComment(
    'The excerpt tag is optional.'
);

$XMLwriterDoc->startElement('excerpt');
$XMLwriterDoc->writeCData('Sherlock Holmes\'s quick eye took
in my occupation, and he shook his head with a smile as he
noticed my questioning glances. "Beyond the obvious facts
that he has at some time done manual labor, that he takes
snuff, that he is a Freemason, that he has been in China,
and that he has done a considerable amount of writing
lately, I can deduce nothing else."');
$XMLwriterDoc->endElement();
$XMLwriterDoc->endElement(); //End book

$XMLwriterDoc->endElement(); //End library

$XMLwriterDoc->endDocument();
```

We could have chosen the more verbose startCData() and startComment() methods, but there's little need in this case. The same calls with the procedural style look like Listing 8.5.

Listing 8.5 library.xml example with XMLWriter, procedural style

```
xmlwriter_write_comment(
    $XMLwriterDoc, 'The excerpt tag is optional.'
);
xmlwriter_start_element($XMLwriterDoc, 'excerpt');

xmlwriter_write_cdata($XMLwriterDoc, 'Sherlock Holmes\'s
quick eye took in my occupation, and he shook his head with
a smile as he noticed my questioning glances. "Beyond the
obvious facts that he has at some time done manual labor,
that he takes snuff, that he is a Freemason, that he has
been in China, and that he has done a considerable amount of
writing lately, I can deduce nothing else."');
xmlwriter_end_element($XMLwriterDoc);
```

Processing Instructions

Recall that processing instructions are directives to an XML reading application and are delimited with <? and ?>, the most familiar of which is the XML document declaration <?xml version="1.0" encoding="utf-8"?>. Another processing instruction you're likely to see is a style sheet declaration. We can add that to the document with writePI().

```
$XMLwriterDoc->writePI(
    'xml-stylesheet', 'type="text/css" href="style.css"'
);
```

Procedural style:

```
xmlwriter_write_pi(
    $XMLwriterDoc,
    'xml-stylesheet',
    'type="text/css" href="style.css"'
);
```

As with most write...() methods, we can accomplish the same task more verbosely with startPI() and endPI().

Raw Text

We mentioned the `writeRaw()` method briefly above, but now let's see what it can really do for us. As the name suggests, `writeRaw()` dumps raw text into your document without any modification. This is the closest XMLWriter comes to editing an existing document. You could load an XML snippet from another library and dump it into your XML document with `writeRaw()`.

You must be cautious, however, as no escaping or character entity translation occurs. Be sure your text is proper XML before passing it to `writeRaw()`. With that warning in mind, let's look at a simple example.

```
$XMLwriterDoc->startElement('book');
$XMLwriterDoc->writeRaw(
    '<title>Firebird: A Trilogy</title>'
);
$XMLwriterDoc->endElement();
```

Notice that the `<title>` tags were passed in their entirety. The same task, procedural style, is as follows:

```
xmlwriter_start_element($XMLwriterDoc,'book');
xmlwriter_write_raw(
    $XMLwriterDoc,
    '<title>Firebird: A Trilogy</title>'
);
xmlwriter_end_element($XMLwriterDoc);
```

The Road Ahead

We have finished our tour of PHP 5 XML libraries. Let's look at more examples of XML in the real world!

Chapter 9

XML in the Wild

We've seen PHP's offerings in SimpleXML, DOM, XMLReader, and XMLWriter. Now we're going to take a brief look at how we can use those libraries with various real-world applications of XML.

Adobe Flex

We've already examined Adobe's MXML language in *Chapter 4* and *Chapter 6*, so I won't go into more detail here. At the heart of all of Adobe's Flash platform is ActionScript, a language based on ECMAScript and therefore very similar to JavaScript. Whether you're creating animations in Flash, applications with the Flex framework, or writing from scratch, all things Flash eventually become ActionScript. As such, MXML is really a language that generates a language. Most MXML tags relate directly to ActionScript objects or data structures, which is helpful to know if you cross languages.

RSS/Atom Syndication

Content syndication feeds are one of the most popular implementations of XML. RSS originally stood for "RDF Site Summary" but is more commonly known as "Really Simple Syndication"[1]. It began as an attempt to provide a "simple" way to produce data feeds of news and other such information published on a given web site.

Today, different standards are used for syndication. The first, known as RSS 0.9, originated at Netscape in March 1999 and was created by Dan Libby and Ramanathan V. Guha. A few months later, Dan Libby updated RSS 0.9 by removing the RDF elements (RDF refers to "Resource Description Framework" and is a W3C recommendation[2]) and incorporating elements of the scriptingNews format by Dave Winer. This second release was called RSS 0.91[3].

Thus began the infighting. RSS forked, with the RSS-DEV community, of which Guha was a member, releasing RSS 1.0, while Winer proposed RSS 0.92, 0.93, 0.94, and finally, 2.0[4].

In an attempt to sidestep the controversy, a third protocol, called Atom, was introduced. However, as none of the protocols after RSS 0.91 had Netscape's involvement, which originally owned and introduced RSS, there's a question as to which, if any, should be the "official" version[5].

Therefore, as of this writing, we who hope to parse a syndication feed may have to contend with one of three protocols: RSS 1.0, RSS 2.0 (which is not a descendant of 1.0), and Atom. So let's talk about something less controversial—like the weather. Here's how we can parse a feed from the Weather Channel[6] using SimpleXML.

[1]   http://en.wikipedia.org/wiki/RSS
[2]   http://www.w3.org/TR/PR-rdf-syntax/
[3]   http://en.wikipedia.org/wiki/RSS
[4]   http://en.wikipedia.org/wiki/RSS
[5]   http://en.wikipedia.org/wiki/RSS
[6]   http://rss.weather.com/weather/rss/local/FRXX0076?cm_ven=LWO&cm_cat=rss&par=LWO_rss

First, an excerpt from the feed is shown in Listing 9.1.

Listing 9.1: RSS Feed Example

```
<?xml version="1.0" encoding="UTF-8"?>
<rss version="2.0">
  <channel>
    <title>The Weather Channel: Your Local Weather Outlook--
Paris, IF (75000)</title>
<link>http://www.weather.com/weather/local/FRXX0076?cm_ven=
LWO&amp;cm_cat=rss&amp;par=LWO_rss&amp;cm_pla=city_page&amp;
cm_ite=cc2&amp;site=city_page</link>
    <description><![CDATA[Local Weather Outlook for Paris,
IF (75000). Since 1982, The Weather Channel has brought
timely weather information to the world.The Weather Channel
...Bringing Weather To Life
]]></description>
    <language><![CDATA[en-us]]></language>
    <copyright><![CDATA[Copyright - 2006, The Weather
Channel Interactive, Inc.]]></copyright>
    <pubDate>Wed, 22 Feb 2012 04:44:54 GMT</pubDate>
    <lastBuildDate>
        Wed, 22 Feb 2012 04:44:54 GMT
    </lastBuildDate>
    <docs>
        <![CDATA[http://blogs.law.harvard.edi/tech/rss]]>
    </docs>
    <ttl>30</ttl>

    <item>
      <guid isPermaLink="false">0.31241940724569683</guid>
      <pubDate>Wed, 22 Feb 2012 04:44:54 GMT</pubDate>
      <title><![CDATA[Current Weather Conditions In Paris,
IF (75000)]]></title>
      <link><![CDATA[http://www.weather.com/weather/local/
FRXX0076?cm_pla=city_page&cm_ite=cc&site=city_page&cm_ven=
LWO&cm_cat=rss&par=LWO_rss]]></link>
      <description><![CDATA[<img src="http://image.weather.
com/web/common/wxicons/31/31.gif?12122006" alt="" />Clear,
and 30 &deg; F. For more details?]]></description>
    </item>

    <item>
      <guid isPermaLink="false">5.426572075698864</guid>
      <pubDate>Wed, 22 Feb 2012 04:44:54 GMT</pubDate>
      <title><![CDATA[Your Weekend Forecast For Paris,
IF (75000)]]></title>
```

```
    <link><![CDATA[http://www.weather.com/weather/weekend/
FRXX0076?cm_ven=LWO&cm_pla=city_page&cm_ite=weekend&site=
city_page&cm_cat=rss&locid=FRXX0076&par=LWO_rss]]></link>
    <description><![CDATA[Chance of Precipitation: Fri:
10% / Sat: 10% / Sun: 10%. For complete forecast details...
]]></description>
    </item>

  </channel>
</rss>
```

The simplest way to get the feed is usihg `file_get_contents`, as long as `allow_url_fopen` is enabled in php.ini. You could, of course, download the feed with curl or another tool.

```
$RSSData = file_get_contents(
    'http://rss.weather.com/weather/rss/local/FRXX0076'
    . '?cm_ven=LWO&cm_cat=rss&par=LWO_rss'
);
```

Next, we'll parse with SimpleXML, see Listing 9.2. Let's suppose that we only care about the city and the current weather so we can insert it into a database for long-term trending. Once we've examined the raw data, we see that we can extract the city from `<title>` and the current weather from one of the `<item>`s.

Listing 9.2: Parsing Weather with SimpleXML

```
$wc = 'The Weather Channel: Your Local Weather Outlook--';
$rss = new SimpleXMLElement($RSSdata);
foreach ($rss->children() as $child) {
  foreach ($child->children() as $grandChild) {
    switch ($grandChild->getName()) {
      case 'title':
        // remove long WC SEO text in title node
        $city = str_replace($wc, '', $grandChild);
        break;

      case 'item':
        // skip if this isn't the current conditions
        if (false === strpos($grandChild->title,
            'Current Weather Conditions')) {
          continue;
        }

        $weather = $grandChild->description;
```

```
         // remove tags, details text, from description
         $weather = preg_replace('/\<.*\>/', '', $weather);
         $weather = str_replace(
                    ' For more details?', '', $weather
                  );
         // replace degree entity
         $weather = str_replace('&deg;', 'deg', $weather);
         break;
    } // Close switch
  }
}

$result[] = array(
    'city' => $city, 'weather' => $weather
);
var_dump($result);
```

Briefly, we create a SimpleXMLElement object from the downloaded RSS data and then loop through each child and grandchild with SimpleXML's children() method. If the tag name of the property, returned by getName(), is either "title" or "item," we want to parse further. A simple str_replace() extracts the city's name from the ‹title› element. ‹item› requires a bit more processing, as we want the one item whose title contains "Current Weather Conditions." Once we've found it, we extract the weather from the item's ‹description› element with a regular expression and a couple more str_replace() calls.

Next, let's look at an example of parsing the same data with DOM, shown in Listing 9.3.

Listing 9.3: Parsing Weather with DOM

```
$DOMdoc = new DOMDocument();
$DOMdoc->loadXML($RSSdata);
$xpath = new DOMXPath($DOMdoc);
// get the channel title
$cityList = $xpath->query('/rss/channel/title');
$city = $cityList->item(0)->nodeValue;
// remove long WC SEO text in title node
$city = str_replace(
    'The Weather Channel: Your Local Weather Outlook--',
    '',
    $city
);
```

```
    // get item nodes
    $itemList = $xpath->query('/rss/channel/item');
    foreach ($itemList as $item) {
        $titleList = $xpath->query('title', $item);
        $descList = $xpath->query('description', $item);
        $count = count($titleList);
        for ($i=0; $i<$count; $i++) {
            // skip if this isn't the current conditions
            if (false === strpos($titleList->item($i)->nodeValue,
              'Current Weather Conditions')) {
                continue;
            }
            $weather = $descList->item($i)->nodeValue;
             // remove tags, details text, from description
            $weather = preg_replace('/\<.*\>/', '', $weather);
            $weather = str_replace(
                            ' For more details?', '', $weather
                    );
            // replace degree entity
            $weather = str_replace('&deg;', 'deg', $weather);
        }
    }
    $result[] = array(
        'city' => $city, 'weather' => $weather
    );
    var_dump($result);
```

The DOM approach is a bit wordier but no less functional. In this case, we create a DOMDocument object, load the RSS data, and create a DOMXPath object to search the RSS data. The query /rss/channel/item allows us to jump right to the ‹title› node, from which we extract the city name with str_replace() just like we did with SimpleXML. Remember that XPath queries always return a DOMNodeList, even if that list has only one element, so we need to access the ‹title› element's data using item(0)->nodeValue.

Next, we get another DOMNodeList of ‹item› elements with the query /rss/channel/item. For each ‹item› element, a relative XPath query, with $item as the context node, allows us to extract DOMNodeLists of the titles and descriptions to see whether they're the nodes we seek. The for loop isn't strictly necessary but is a good failsafe in case the feed on another day throws us a curve. Once we've found the current weather conditions, we extract them from $descList by again dereferencing with the item($i)->$nodeValue property and clean them up just like the SimpleXML example above.

Finally, let's parse the same data with XMLReader.

Listing 9.4: Parsing Weather with XMLReader

```php
$XMLDoc = new XMLReader();
$XMLDoc->xml($RSSdata, 'utf-8', LIBXML_NOBLANKS);
$wc = 'The Weather Channel: Your Local Weather Outlook--';
while ($XMLDoc->read()) {
   if ($XMLDoc->name == 'title') {
       // remove long WC SEO text in title node
       $city = str_replace(
                   $wc, '', $XMLDoc->readInnerXML()
               );
       break;
   }
} // Close while

while ($XMLDoc->next()) {
  if ($XMLDoc->name == 'item') {
      // skip if this item is not the current conditions
      if (false === strpos($XMLDoc->readString(),
              'Current Weather Conditions')) {
          continue;
      }

      // walk through the data
      while ($XMLDoc->read()) {
          // check if we are in <description>
          if ($XMLDoc->name == 'description' &&
              $XMLDoc->readOuterXML() != '<description/>') {

              $weather = $XMLDoc->readString();

              // remove tags, details text, from description
              $weather = preg_replace(
                          '/\<.*\>/', '', $weather
                      );
              $weather = str_replace(
                          ' For more details?', '', $weather
                      );
              // replace degree entity
              $weather = str_replace('&deg;', 'deg', $weather);
              break 2;
          }
      }
  }
}
$XMLDoc->close();
$result = array(
    'city' => $city, 'weather' => $weather
);
var_dump($result);
```

With XMLReader, as we already have the RSS data in a string, we'll load it with the xml() method rather than open(). Next, we walk through the data with read() until we find the <title> node and extract the data just like the SimpleXML example. Because we know the <title> node and <item> nodes are siblings, we can break out of the first while loop and iterate through sibling nodes with next() for faster parsing. Once we find an item node, we dump the entire node contents as a string with readString() and pass that to strpos() to ensure we have the node we want. If so, a final while loop with read() steps us through each node until we find the description and extract it as we did with SimpleXML. Notice I also included the check for <description/>. If the loop were to continue, it would hit the closing description tag and overwrite our variable with a blank string. However, to save time and avoid the risk of another node's matching our strpos() check, we can break out of both while loops at once with break 2.

I generally prefer the SimpleXML approach, both because it requires fewer lines of code and because it requires less prior knowledge of the document's structure. I do not even need to know the root node's name in order to start walking through the downloaded data with SimpleXML. DOM's lack of a method like SimpleXML's children() forces us to fall back on XPath wildcard queries and can be a liability when dealing with unknown or obfuscated documents.

SOAP and WSDL

SOAP originally meant "Simple Object Access Protocol." But it is no longer an acronym and is just a terminology used for this technolog.[7]. It is a technique of defining functions that can be called remotely over a network like the Internet, that is, remote procedure calls via a standard protocol, usually HTTP[8]. In recent years, SOAP has fallen in popularity in favor of REST due to the higher processing overhead and the complexity of defining SOAP messages. SOAP messages, both request and response, are encoded in XML.

To further our use of SOAP, we can publish details about our SOAP functions and data structures via Web Services Description Language, or WSDL. WSDL is another XML-based language[9].

[7]   http://www.w3.org/TR/soap12-part1/#intro
[8]   http://www.w3schools.com/webservices/ws_soap_intro.asp
[9]   http://www.w3schools.com/wsdl/wsdl_documents.asp

Let's define, via SOAP, and publish, via WSDL, a web service for getting a title from an ISBN for our `library.xml` document.

First, our WSDL interface shown in Listing 9.5.

Listing 9.5: WSDL interface

```
<?xml version="1.0" encoding="UTF-8"?>
<definitions name="getTitleService"
    targetNamespace="http://www.libraryexample.com/booklist"
    xmlns="http://schemas.xmlsoap.org/wsdl/"
    xmlns:soap="http://schemas.xmlsoap.org/wsdl/soap/"
    xmlns:ex="http://www.libraryexample.com/booklist"
    xmlns:xs="http://www.w3.org/2001/XMLSchema">

    <message name="getTitleRequest">
        <part name="ISBN" type="xs:string"/>
    </message>
    <message name="getTitleResponse">
        <part name="Title" type="xs:string"/>
    </message>

    <portType name="TitlePortType">
        <operation name="getTitle">
            <input message="ex:getTitleRequest"/>
            <output message="ex:getTitleResponse"/>
        </operation>
    </portType>

    <binding name="TitleBinding" type="ex:TitlePortType">
        <soap:binding style="rpc" transport="http://schemas.xmlsoap.
org/soap/http"/>
        <operation name="getTitle">
            <soap:operation soapAction="getTitle"/>
            <input>
                <soap:body
                    encodingStyle="http://schemas.xmlsoap.org/soap/
encoding/"
                    use="encoded"/>
            </input>
            <output>
                <soap:body
                    encodingStyle="http://schemas.xmlsoap.org/soap/
encoding/"
                    use="encoded"/>
            </output>
        </operation>
    </binding>
```

```
    <service name="getTitleService">
        <documentation>WSDL File for getTitleService</documentation>
        <port binding="ex:TitleBinding" name="TitlePort">
            <soap:address location="http://localhost:8080/soap/
servlet/rpcrouter"/>
        </port>
    </service>
</definitions>
```

A WSDL interface usually sits on a server waiting for users to call it, so there's little need to generate it dynamically with PHP. The WSDL format can be complicated and difficult to write, so there are a number of generators available on the internet.

We can create a SOAP request for this WSDL using SimpleXML as in Listing 9.6.

Listing 9.6: Creating a SOAP request with SimpleXML

```
$SOAPstring = '<?xml version="1.0"?>
<soap:envelope
xmlns:soap="http://www.w3.org/2001/12/soap-envelope"
soap:encodingStyle="http://www.w3.org/2001/12/soap-encoding">
</soap:envelope>';
$SOAP = new SimpleXMLElement($SOAPstring);

$body = $SOAP->addChild('soap:body');
$getTitle = $body->addChild(
    'l:getTitle',
    null,
    'http://www.libraryexample.com/booklist'
);
$ISBN = $getTitle->addChild('l:ISBN', '0765328321');

echo $SOAP->asXML();
```

The tags that appear within the <soap:body> tag are application-specific tags, in our case <l:getTitle> and <l:ISBN>. As you can see, we defined our own namespace for our application with the "l" (lower case "L", as in "Library") for those application-specific tags.

The SOAP response might look something like this:

```
$SOAPresponse = '<?xml version="1.0"?>
<soap:Envelope
  xmlns:soap="http://www.w3.org/2001/12/soap-envelope"
  soap:encodingStyle="http://www.w3.org/2001/12/soap-encoding"
>
<soap:Body>
   <l:getTitleResponse
        xmlns:l="http://www.libraryexample.com/booklist">
      <l:Title>Halo: The Fall of Reach</l:Title>
   </l:getTitleResponse>
</soap:Body>
</soap:Envelope>';
```

And we can parse out the title with a simple XPath query.

```
$SOAP = new SimpleXMLElement($SOAPresponse);
$SOAP->registerXPathNamespace(
    'l', 'http://www.libraryexample.com/booklist'
);
$titleArray = $SOAP->xpath('//l:Title');
$title = $titleArray[0];
echo (string)$title;
```

REST

Some programmers are confused about what REST actually is. REST is neither a protocol like SOAP nor a language like XHTML, but rather it is a series of principles for creating lean, efficient data sources that can be accessed over a distributed network like the Internet. Services that conform to REST principles are generally referred to as being "RESTful." REST stands for "REpresentational State Transfer" and was originally outlined by Roy Fielding[10]. REST does not have to be implemented in XML, but XML is a common way to publish RESTful data.

The generally accepted principles that make a web service RESTful are:

- A global identifier. (Usually a URI)
- Atomic transactions (i.e., the server does not maintain state)
- The requesting application and the answering server need know nothing about the network in between. (This is typically accomplished by using the http:// protocol.)
- The requesting application must understand the representation of data returned, be it XML, HTML, JSON, an image, and so on.

[10]   *http://www.ics.uci.edu/~fielding/pubs/dissertation/rest_arch_style.htm*

Thus, to access a REST interface, we could call a URI with some HTTP GET variables, as in:

```
http://www.example.com/library.php?ISBN=0765328321
```

To respond, we'd simply generate an XML document fragment with the requested data. Assuming we already have a DOMDocument and DOMXPath object, we could respond with:

```php
$ISBN = (int)$_GET['ISBN']; // Sanitize user data
$nodeList = $xpath->query(
    '/library/book[@ISBN="'.$ISBN.'"]'
);
$book = $nodeList->item(0);
$bookDoc = new DOMDocument('1.0', 'utf-8');
$bookNode = $bookDoc->importNode($book, true);
$bookDoc->appendChild($bookNode);
echo $bookDoc->saveXML();
```

Note that we have to create a new DOMDocument, $bookDoc, and import the $book node to echo it back as XML. Simply echoing $book would have given us the raw data without XML tags.

With REST, the receiving application merely needs to know that it is receiving data in XML format. We do not need to conform to a specific document definition like we do with SOAP. Note also that it is possible, though less common, to publish the details of a REST interface with WSDL.

XHTML

XHTML was an attempt to recreate HTML as pure XML. Had the effort been successful, it might have made parsing web pages and scraping data easier, but there's a great deal of sloppy code out there (admittedly, I've written some of it.) Strict adherence to XML standards would have broken web pages, Internet Explorer was slow in supporting XHTML[11], and a large number of developers simply never moved to the standard. As such, XHTML as an independent language has been abandoned in favor of HTML5[12].

Therefore, we won't spend much time on XHTML, but there's still enough of it out there to justify a quick parsing example, shown in Listing 9.7.

[11]   *http://blogs.msdn.com/b/ie/archive/2005/09/15/467901.aspx*
[12]   *http://www.w3.org/2009/06/xhtml-faq.html*

Listing 9.7: XHTML Parsing

```php
<?php
$XHTML = <<<END_OF_XHTML
<!DOCTYPE html
    PUBLIC "-_W3C_DTD XHTML 1.0 Strict//EN"
    "http://www.w3.org/TR/xhtml1/DTD/xhtml1-strict.dtd">
<html xmlns="http://www.w3.org/1999/xhtml"
      xml:lang="en" lang="en">
    <head>
        <title>Gettysburg Address</title>
    </head>
    <body>
        <p>Four score and seven years ago our fathers brought
forth on this continent, a new nation, conceived in Liberty,
and dedicated to the proposition that all men are created
equal.</p>
        <p>Now we are engaged in a great civil war, testing
whether that nation, or any nation so conceived and so
dedicated, can long endure. We are met on a great
battlefield of that war. We have come to dedicate a portion
of that field, as a final resting place for those who here
gave their lives that that nation might live. It is
altogether fitting and proper that we should do this.</p>
    </body>
</html>
END_OF_XHTML;

$XHTML = '<?xml version="1.0" encoding="utf8"?>'
        . "\n" . $XHTML;

$DOMdoc = new DOMDocument();
$DOMdoc->loadXML($XHTML);
$xpath = new DOMXPath($DOMdoc);
$xpath->registerNamespace(
    'x', 'http://www.w3.org/1999/xhtml'
);
$nodeList = $xpath->query('//x:p');
foreach ($nodeList as $node) {
    echo "$node->nodeValue\n\n";
}
```

Pretty simple, but there are a couple of items worth highlighting. First, many
XHTML 1.x documents do not include the `<?xml ?>` declaration at the top,
so you would need to add it. Current versions of DOM and SimpleXML will
forgive you if you overlook it, but it's a best practice to add it.

Second, notice the call to $xpath->registerNamespace(). There isn't an x prefix in the document, so where did that come from? If you recall from *Chapter 4*, even default namespaces must be declared to XPath. Because there is no prefix associated with the default namespace, I arbitrarily chose x. That makes our XPath query _x:p mean "give me all p tags in the default namespace." Had we simply used _p, we would have gotten no results, as XHTML does not have "namespaceless" tags.

Here's the same exercise with SimpleXML:

```
$gettysburg = new SimpleXMLElement($XHTML);
$gettysburg->registerXPathNamespace(
    'x', 'http://www.w3.org/1999/xhtml'
);
$nodeList = $gettysburg->xpath('//x:p');
foreach ($nodeList as $node) {
    echo "$node\n\n";
}
```

The Gettysburg Address is courtesy of the Abraham Lincoln Association[13].

Creating an RSS Feed

Let's load the data from our library.xml file in a multidimensional array called $books. (I am omitting the <excerpt> tag for brevity.) Then, using that data, we'll produce a simple RSS 2.0 feed that displays a random "book of the day."

Loading the Data

Listing 9.8 shows how to read the data with SimpleXML. Note we pass in the path to our file to the constructor and then easily loop through the book items using foreach. Since $row is a SimpleXMLElement, to get the value for use later you have to cast it to a string, or another scalar type.

---

[13]   Collected Works of Abraham Lincoln, edited by Roy P. Basler. *http://phpa.me/ALAGettysburgAddress*

Listing 9.8: Loading `library.xml` with SimpleXML

```php
$lib = new SimpleXMLElement('library.xml', null, true);
$books = array();
foreach ($lib->children() as $child) {
    $book = array('ISBN' => (string)$child['ISBN']);
    foreach ($child->children() as $row) {
        $key = $row->getName();
        if ($key == 'excerpt') {
            continue;
        }
        $book[$key] = (string)$row;
    }
    $books[] = $book;
}
```

Generating an RSS feed

Listing 9.9 returns the RSS feed, building the response with plain PHP strings.

An RSS feed's root tag is, predictably, ‹rss›. Be sure to include the version attribute because parsing RSS can differ significantly between versions, as described above. After that comes the ‹channel› tag, which describes the specific feed. Each ‹channel› requires a ‹title›, ‹link› and ‹description› element. You can then have as many ‹item› elements as you like; each also requires a ‹title›, ‹link›, and ‹description›.

We also added a couple of recommended features. Within the ‹item› tag there is a ‹guid›—a globally unique identifier, which can often be identical to the ‹link› tag, so long as it points to this specific item rather than to the feed itself. Second, we added an ‹atom:link› tag to make this feed friendlier to Atom readers.

Listing 9.9: Create a feed with strings

```php
<?php
$RSS = '<?xml version="1.0" encoding="utf-8"?>
<rss version="2.0" xmlns:atom="http://www.w3.org/2005/Atom">
    <channel>
        <title>Book of the Day</title>
        <link>http://www.libraryexample.org/RSSbook.php</link>
        <atom:link xmlns:atom="http://www.w3.org/2005/Atom"
            href="http://www.libraryexample.org/RSSbook.php"
            rel="self" type="application/rss+xml" />
        <description>
            A random book from a very small library.
        </description>
        <item>';

$i = rand(0, count($books)-1);

$link = 'http://www.libraryexample.org/book.php'
    . '?ISBN=' . $books[$i]['ISBN'];
$RSS .= "
    <title>{$books[$i]['title']}</title>
    <link>{$link}</link>
    <guid>{$link}</guid>
    <description>
        {$books[$i]['title']} by {$books[$i]['author']}.
        {$books[$i]['format']}, {$books[$i]['pages']} pages.
        Published by {$books[$i]['publisher']},
        in {$books[$i]['year']}.
    </description>";

$RSS .= '
        </item>
    </channel>
</rss>';
echo $RSS;
```

SimpleXML

In Listing 9.10, we see how to build an RSS feed using SimpleXML's functionality. For every tag we need, we use the addChild method to create it and add it to the correct parent. Similarly, addAttribute sets any attributes needed for a tag. Note that for the atom:link tag, the value in addChild is null because the url is specified via the href attribute.

Listing 9.10: RSS feed built with SimpleXML

```php
<?php
$RSSstring = '<?xml version="1.0" encoding="utf-8"?>
<rss version="2.0" xmlns:atom="http://www.w3.org/2005/Atom">
</rss>';
$RSS = new SimpleXMLElement($RSSstring);
// create our channel element with title, link,
// description, and atom:link items
$channel = $RSS->addChild('channel');
$title = $channel->addChild('title', 'Book of the Day');
$link = $channel->addChild(
    'link', 'http://www.libraryexample.org/RSSbook.php'
);
$desc = $channel->addChild(
    'description',
    'A random book from a very small library.'
);
$atomLink = $channel->addChild(
    'atom:link', null, 'http://www.w3.org/2005/Atom'
);
$atomLink->addAttribute(
    'href', 'http://www.libraryexample.org/RSSbook.php'
);
$atomLink->addAttribute('rel', 'self');
$atomLink->addAttribute('type', 'application/rss+xml');
// select a random book form our array
$i = rand(0, count($books)-1);
// add the book as an item
$item = $channel->addChild('item');
// add the title node for our book
$item->addChild('title', $books[$i]['title']);
// generate book url, add it as link and guid nodes
$link = 'http://www.libraryexample.org/book.php'
        . '?ISBN=' . $books[$i]['ISBN'];
$item->addChild('link', $link);
$item->addChild('guid', $link);
// format and add a description node
$description = "
{$books[$i]['title']} by {$books[$i]['author']}.
{$books[$i]['format']}, {$books[$i]['pages']} pages.
Published by {$books[$i]['publisher']},
in {$books[$i]['year']}";
$desc = $item->addChild('description', $description);
// output the RSS XML
echo $RSS->asXML();
```

DOM

We can also use DOM to build the RSS feed, as in Listing 9.11. As always, the important thing to remember with DOM is to append the DOMElement *before* modifying it. Notice how we appended $atomLink before adding attributes.

Listing 9.11: RSS feed built with DOM

```
$RSS = new DOMDocument('1.0', 'utf-8');
$RSS->formatOutput = true;
$RSStag = new DOMElement('rss');
$RSS->appendChild($RSStag);
$RSStag->setAttribute('version', '2.0');
$RSStag->setAttribute(
    'xmlns:atom', 'http://www.w3.org/2005/Atom'
);
// create our channel element
$channel = new DOMElement('channel');
$RSStag->appendChild($channel);
// add title, link, and description tags
$title = new DOMElement('title', 'Book of the Day');
$link = new DOMElement(
    'link', 'http://www.libraryexample.org/RSSbook.php'
);
$desc = new DOMElement(
    'description',
    'A random book from a very small library.'
);
$channel->appendChild($title);
$channel->appendChild($link);
$channel->appendChild($desc);
// create atomLink element and add it to the channel
$atomLink = new DOMElement(
    'atom:link', null, 'http://www.w3.org/2005/Atom'
);
$channel->appendChild($atomLink);
$atomLink->setAttribute(
    'href', 'http://www.libraryexample.org/RSSbook.php'
);
$atomLink->setAttribute('rel', 'self');
$atomLink->setAttribute('type', 'application/rss+xml');
// select a random book form our array
$i = rand(0, count($books)-1);
// add the book as an item
$item = new DOMElement('item');
$channel->appendChild($item);
// put the book title into a title element
```

```php
$itemTitle = new DOMElement('title', $books[$i]['title']);
// generate book url, add it as link and guid nodes
$link = 'http://www.libraryexample.org/book.php'
        . '?ISBN=' . $books[$i]['ISBN'];
$itemLink = new DOMElement('link', $link);
$itemGUID = new DOMElement('guid', $link);
// add title, link, guid to parent item
$item->appendChild($itemTitle);
$item->appendChild($itemLink);
$item->appendChild($itemGUID);
// format and add a description element
$description = "
{$books[$i]['title']} by {$books[$i]['author']}.
{$books[$i]['format']}, {$books[$i]['pages']} pages.
Published by {$books[$i]['publisher']},
in {$books[$i]['year']}";
$itemDesc = new DOMElement('description', $description);
$item->appendChild($itemDesc);
// output the RSS XML
echo $RSS->saveXML();
```

XMLWriter

Finally, in Listing 9.12 we use XMLWriter to generate our RSS feed. XMLWriter is a bit more verbose than the other examples are, but remember it operates as a stream, which preserves memory. There are some things to notice about this example. First, we opened php://stdout. If this script is executed by a web server, stdout may well point to its output stream. You may have to adjust your open() call based on the server you use. Second, defining the atom namespace in the <rss> tag used a call to writeAttribute(), not writeAttributeNS(). This is because we didn't want to apply the atom: namespace to the attribute itself, nor did we want to apply it to the <rss> tag. We actually used the defined namespace with a call to startElementNS() a little later when we created the <atom:link> tag. Finally, notice the interplay of startElement() and writeElement() to keep the code as clean as possible.

Listing 9.12: RSS feed built with XMLWriter

```php
$XMLwriterDoc = new XMLWriter();
$XMLwriterDoc->openURI('php://stdout');
$XMLwriterDoc->startDocument('1.0','utf-8');
// tell output to indent with tabs
$XMLwriterDoc->setIndentString("\t");
$XMLwriterDoc->setIndent(true);
// create our root element
$XMLwriterDoc->startElement('rss');
$XMLwriterDoc->writeAttribute('version', '2.0');
$XMLwriterDoc->writeAttribute(
    'xmlns:atom', 'http://www.w3.org/2005/Atom'
);
// create our channel element
$XMLwriterDoc->startElement('channel');
// add title, link, and description tags
$XMLwriterDoc->writeElement('title', 'Book of the Day');
$XMLwriterDoc->writeElement(
    'link', 'http://www.libraryexample.org/RSSbook.php'
);
$XMLwriterDoc->writeElement(
    'description', 'A random book from a very small library.'
);
// create atomLink element and add it to the channel
$XMLwriterDoc->startElementNS(
    'atom', 'link', 'http://www.w3.org/2005/Atom'
);
$XMLwriterDoc->writeAttribute(
    'href', 'http://www.libraryexample.org/RSSbook.php'
);
$XMLwriterDoc->writeAttribute('rel', 'self');
$XMLwriterDoc->writeAttribute(
    'type', 'application/rss+xml'
);
$XMLwriterDoc->endElement();
// select a random book form our array
$i = rand(0, count($books)-1);
// format a description
$description = "
{$books[$i]['title']} by {$books[$i]['author']}.
{$books[$i]['format']}, {$books[$i]['pages']} pages.
Published by {$books[$i]['publisher']},
in {$books[$i]['year']}";
// build the link to this book
$link = 'http://www.libraryexample.org/book.php'
    . '?ISBN=' . $books[$i]['ISBN'];
```

```
// create an item element to hold our book
$XMLwriterDoc->startElement('item');
// add the title, link, and guid elements
$XMLwriterDoc->writeElement('title', $books[$i]['title'])
$XMLwriterDoc->writeElement('link', $link);
$XMLwriterDoc->writeElement('guid', $link);
// add the description
$XMLwriterDoc->writeElement('description', $description);
$XMLwriterDoc->endElement(); //End item
$XMLwriterDoc->endElement(); //End channel
$XMLwriterDoc->endElement(); //End rss
$XMLwriterDoc->endDocument();
```

Turning a Database Resultset into XML

Database resultsets are two-dimensional arrays. Here's a generic ResultSet-to-XML function I use frequently, especially to respond to Ajax and Action Message Format (ActionScript) calls.

```
$resultSet = $mysqli->query("SELECT * FROM table");
$XML = '<?xml version="1.0" encoding="utf-8"?>
<root>
</root>';
$XMLobj = new SimpleXMLElement($XML);
while ($row = $resultSet->fetch_assoc()) {
    $record = $XMLobj->addChild('record');
    foreach ($row as $key=>$value) {
        $record->addChild($key, htmlentities($value));
    }
}
echo $XMLobj->asXML();
```

Which is Better?

We've seen how do create a number of common XML document types with both SimpleXML and DOM. That raises the question: which one should you use? Is one better than the other for a certain application? Possibly one of the most significant factors is memory usage. DOM has a dramatically larger memory footprint than does SimpleXML[14]. So to keep your applications lean and efficient, it is usually preferable to use SimpleXML. My rule of thumb is use SimpleXML whenever possible, convert to DOM for those advanced features that require it, and convert back to SimpleXML to continue processing.

[14]   http://svn.bitflux.org/repos/public/php5examples/largexml/fulldocu.pdf

The Road Ahead

There is little left on our XML journey. The one remaining stop is that of XML validation—making sure your documents play well with others.

Chapter
10

Validation

We mentioned way back in *Chapter 1* that an XML document should be *well formed* and *valid*. Well formed refers to the structure of the document and applies to every XML document, from the simplest to the most complex. Valid, on the other hand, requires a stricter external definition of what makes the form of a particular group of documents correct. The process of checking the *correctness* of an XML document against an external source is called *validation*.

The most common XML validation document is a *Document Type Definition* or DTD. DTDs are a holdover from XML's parent language, SGML[1]. You're probably familiar with DTDs, as they are often declared at the top of HTML pages. A DTD defines the structure, and lists the legal elements and attributes for an XML document. Using and validating against a standard DTD allows separate groups of people to interchange data in an agreed upon format.

[1]   XML in Theory and Practice, by Chris Bates, p. 43

DTDs, however, are a language unto themselves. "Why can't we validate XML with XML?" some asked. So XML Schema was born[2]. An XML Schema validation document is indeed pure XML, but the requirements of writing the document can be as complex as writing a DTD.

Several other validation schemes have been proposed in attempts to simplify XML validation. The details of how to write each of these validation methods have been covered extensively in several other books by other, so I will defer to them. Of these validation methods, DOM and XMLReader offer support for DTD, XML Schema, and RelaxNG. In this chapter, we'll cover how to validate your documents with both. Neither SimpleXML nor XMLWriter offers validation methods.

Document Type Definitions

A Document Type Definition describes how an XML document is structures via element and attribute-list declarations. These lists declare the allowable elements (or tags), and the allowable set and type of attributes for each declared element. To learn more about creating a DTD see *DTD Tutorial*[3] and the DTD specification[4] itself.

In practice, most programmers will use an existing Document Type Definition to validate an XML document, hence we won't go into how to create one. DOM offers one DTD validation function, which assumes the DTD has already been declared in your document. For example, if we were to validate an XHTML file, we could simply call `validate()` against the loaded DOMDocument object. The first line in any XML file must be the `<?xml ?>` declaration, so to validate a simple XHTML document like the one below, we have to be sure to add that at the top.

---

[2]   XML in Theory and Practice, by Chris Bates, p. 61
[3]   *http://www.w3schools.com/dtd/*
[4]   *http://www.w3.org/XML/1998/06/xmlspec-report-v21.htm*

```php
$XHTML = <<<EOT
<?xml version="1.0" encoding="UTF-8"?>
<!DOCTYPE html PUBLIC "-_W3C_DTD XHTML 1.0 Strict//EN"
   "http://www.w3.org/TR/xhtml1/DTD/xhtml1-strict.dtd">
<html xmlns="http://www.w3.org/1999/xhtml" xml:lang="en">
    <head>
        <title>XHTML 1.0 Strict Example</title>
    </head>
    <body>
        <p>This is an example of an XHTML 1.0
            Strict document.</p>
    </body>
</html>
EOT;

$DOMdoc = new DOMDocument();
$DOMdoc->loadXML($XHTML);
if ($DOMdoc->validate()) {
    echo "Document is valid.";
}
```

Validation requires the system to download the DTD over a network connection, so you must run it from a computer that is connected. The speed of validation will be affected by your connection speed. Remember, that if you need to validate a SimpleXML document you must convert it to a DOMDocument first.

Let's try the same process with XMLReader. Like DOM, XMLReader will validate against the DTD that has already been declared in your document. However, rather than load the data as a stream with XMLReader::xml(), let's open a file, as reading a data stream from a file is a more realistic application of XMLReader. Let's imagine we've saved the example above in a file called XHTML_test.html.

```php
$XMLreaderDoc = new XMLReader();
$XMLreaderDoc->open('XHTML_test.html');
$XMLreaderDoc->setParserProperty(XMLReader::VALIDATE, true);
if ($XMLreaderDoc->isValid() {
    echo "Document is valid.";
)
$XMLreaderDoc->close();
```

Notice the setParserProperty() call before calling isValid(). This is a requirement for validating against DTDs, as by default XMLReader does not validate while it reads. This makes sense because validating requires additional overhead that streaming applications will generally want to avoid.

Another gotcha is that XMLReader will only validate the node that it currently has in memory. For small documents like ours, it may well validate the entire document, but for large documents, you will need to either call isValid() on each node or read to the end of the document and trap validation errors.

XML Schema

XML Schema provides a different method for describing the structure of XML documents that aims to be a simpler and clearer way to define the allowed datatypes, elements, content, and attributes. For more information, see the W3C's XML Schema specification[5]. An XML Schema itself is an XML Document that uses elements and attributes in the xs namespace to define how an XML document can be written. To learn how to write an XML Schema see *XML Schema Tutorial*[6].

Unlike the DTD validate() function in DOM or isValid() in XMLReader, XML Schema validation requires you to load a separate validation document. For DOM, like most of its methods, this comes in two flavors: schemaValidate() for loading from disk and schemaValidateSource() for using a string that has already been loaded.

[5]   *http://www.w3.org/TR/xmlschema11-1/*
[6]   *http://www.w3schools.com/schema/default.asp*

Listing 10.1: An XML Schema file

```xml
<?xml version="1.0" encoding="utf-8"?>
<xsd:schema xmlns:xsd="http://www.w3.org/2001/XMLSchema">
    <xsd:element name="library">
        <xsd:complexType>
            <xsd:sequence>
                <xsd:element name="book" maxOccurs="unbounded">
                    <xsd:complexType>
                        <xsd:sequence>
                            <xsd:element name="title"
                                         type="xsd:string"
                                         maxOccurs="1"/>
                            <xsd:element name="author"
                                         type="xsd:string"
                                         maxOccurs="1"/>
                            <xsd:element name="pages"
                                         type="xsd:positiveInteger"
                                         maxOccurs="1"/>
                            <xsd:element name="format"
                                         type="xsd:string"
                                         maxOccurs="1"/>
                            <xsd:element name="publisher"
                                         type="xsd:string"
                                         maxOccurs="1"/>
                            <xsd:element name="year"
                                         type="xsd:string"
                                         maxOccurs="1"/>
                            <xsd:element name="language"
                                         type="xsd:string"
                                         maxOccurs="1"/>
                            <xsd:element name="excerpt"
                                         type="xsd:string"
                                         minOccurs="0"/>
                        </xsd:sequence>
                        <xsd:attribute name="id"
                                       type="xsd:string"
                                       use="required"/>
                        <xsd:attribute name="ISBN"
                                       type="xsd:string"
                                       use="required"/>
                    </xsd:complexType>
                </xsd:element>
            </xsd:sequence>
        </xsd:complexType>
    </xsd:element>
</xsd:schema>
```

An XML Schema document for our `library.xml` file might look something like Listing 10.1, stored in a file named `schema.xml`. Validating it with DOM would require the following.

```
$DOMdoc = new DOMDocument();
$DOMdoc->load('library.xml');
if ($DOMdoc->schemaValidate('schema.xml')) {
    echo "Document is valid.";
}
```

XMLReader offers a similar method for validating against XML Schema: setSchema(). You will need to pass the filepath to your XML Schema document to setSchema() *after* calling XMLReader::open() but *before* calling XMLReader::read(). Validating it with XMLReader is shown below. It is not necessary to set XMLReader::VALIDATE to true when using XML Schema. By default, XML Schema returns validation failures as PHP warnings. However, you can use the libxml_use_internal_errors and libxml_get_last_error to handle any errors.

```
$XMLreaderDoc = new XMLReader();
$XMLreaderDoc->open('library.xml');
$XMLreaderDoc->setSchema('schema.xml');
libxml_use_internal_errors(TRUE);
while ($XMLreaderDoc->read()) {
    if (!$XMLreaderDoc->isValid()) {
        $err = libxml_get_last_error();
        echo 'Line ' . $err->line . ': ' . $err->message;
        break;
    }
}
$XMLreaderDoc->close();
```

RelaxNG

RelaxNG (REgular LAnguage for XML Next Generation) is one of the attempts to simplify XML validation documents, and the details can be found at *http://www.relaxng.org*. The standard actually defines two validation languages: one in pure XML, and a shorter, more cryptic form for those who prefer minified documents. Compared the DTDs and XML Schemas it is relatively simple, and at its core uses patterns to match and describe what elements and attributes are allowed. For more about RelaxNG, see Eric van der Vlists' book on RELAXNG [7].

[7]   *http://books.xmlschemata.org/relaxng/page2.html*

Listing 10.2: Simple RelaxNG XML file

```xml
<?xml version="1.0" encoding="utf-8"?>
<rng:element name="library"
            xmlns:rng="http://relaxng.org/ns/structure/1.0">
    <rng:zeroOrMore>
        <rng:element name="book">
            <rng:attribute name="id">
                <text/>
            </rng:attribute>
            <rng:attribute name="ISBN">
                <text/>
            </rng:attribute>
            <rng:zeroOrMore>
                <rng:element name="title">
                    <rng:text/>
                </rng:element>
                <rng:element name="author">
                    <rng:text/>
                </rng:element>
                <rng:element name="pages">
                    <rng:text/>
                </rng:element>
                <rng:element name="format">
                    <rng:text/>
                </rng:element>
                <rng:element name="publisher">
                    <rng:text/>
                </rng:element>
                <rng:element name="year">
                    <rng:text/>
                </rng:element>
                <rng:element name="language">
                    <rng:text/>
                </rng:element>
                <rng:optional>
                    <rng:element name="excerpt">
                        <rng:text/>
                    </rng:element>
                </rng:optional>
            </rng:zeroOrMore>
        </rng:element>
    </rng:zeroOrMore>
</rng:element>
```

RelaxNG validation with DOM follows the same pattern as XML Schema: `relaxNGValidate()` to load a validation file and `relaxNGValidateSource()` to validate against a preloaded string. A simplified RelaxNG schema in XML format is shown in Listing 10.2. Validating against it, assuming it is saved as `relaxng.xml` is shown below.

```
$DOMdoc = new DOMDocument();
$DOMdoc->load('library.xml');
$schema = file_get_contents('relaxng.xml');
$DOMdoc->load('library.xml');
if ($DOMdoc->relaxNGValidateSource($schema)) {
    echo "Document is valid.";
}
```

XMLReader offers two methods for validating against RelaxNG that parallel DOM's methods: `setRelaxNGSchema()` to load a RelaxNG schema file and `setRelaxNGSchemaSource()` to load a string. As with `setSchema()`, you will need to set your RelaxNG schema *after* calling `open()` but *before* calling `read()`.

Like XML Schema, it is not necessary to set `XMLReader::VALIDATE` to true when using RelaxNG. Also like XML Schema, RelaxNG will return validation failures as PHP warnings, unless you manually handle them.

```
$XMLreaderDoc = new XMLReader();
$XMLreaderDoc->open('library.xml');
$XMLreaderDoc->setRelaxNGSchema('relaxng.xml');

libxml_use_internal_errors(TRUE);
while ($XMLreaderDoc->read()) {
    if (!$XMLreaderDoc->isValid()) {
        $err = libxml_get_last_error();
        echo 'Line ' . $err->line . ': ' . $err->message;
        break;
    }
}
$XMLreaderDoc->close();
```

End of the Road

Congratulations! You now have a grasp of what is possible with XML. PHP offers a powerful set of tools for parsing XML and putting it to use. Unleash that XML on the world!

Appendix
A

SimpleXML Function Reference

SimpleXML is an Object-Oriented library, so there are few procedural functions. As such, most method calls are to a `SimpleXMLElement` object.

Method signatures come from the PHP online manual at _http://php.net/simplexml_, but I have attempted to test each method and to fill in the gaps when the PHP online manual is incomplete or ambiguous. Please refer to the online manual for the most complete and up-to-date information.

Note that the iterative properties of `SimpleXMLElement` methods can prevent the returned object from being viewed with `print_r()`, `var_dump()` or anything else that can examine objects. Results may vary with different debuggers.

SimpleXMLElement Methods

__construct()

```
SimpleXMLElement __construct( string $data
    [, int $options = 0 [, bool $data_is_url = false
    [, string $ns = "" [, bool $is_prefix = false ]]]] )
```

__construct() creates a new SimpleXMLElement object. It is invoked with the new operator.

Tips

Use libxml_use_internal_errors() to suppress all XML errors, and libxml_get_errors() to iterate over them afterwards.

Example

```
$myXML = new SimpleXMLElement(
    '/path/to/my/file.xml', null, true
);
```

addAttribute()

```
void addAttribute ( string $name [, string $value
    [, string $namespace ]] )
```

addAttribute() adds an attribute (a quoted key/value pair) to the SimpleXMLElement on which it's invoked.

Example

```
$childNode->addAttribute('username', 'jsmith');
```

addChild()

```
SimpleXMLElement addChild ( string $name [, string $value
    [, string $namespace ]] )
```

addChild() Adds a child element to the node on which it's invoked and returns a SimpleXMLElement of the child.

Example

```
$bookNode->addChild('title','Halo: The Fall of Reach');
```

asXML()

```
mixed asXML([ string $filename ] )
```

The asXML method formats the parent object's data in XML version 1.0.

Example

```
$rawXMLstring = $myXMLnode->asXML();
```

attributes()

```
SimpleXMLElement attributes([ string $ns = NULL
    [, bool $is_prefix = false ]] )
```

attributes() returns a SimpleXML object of key/value pairs representing the attributes and values defined within a single XML tag.

Example

```
$myXMLattr = $myXMLnode->attributes();
```

children()

```
SimpleXMLElement children([ string $ns
    [, bool $is_prefix = false ]] )
```

children() returns a SimpleXMLElement representing the child nodes of the element on which it's invoked.

Example

```
foreach ($myXML->children() as $child) { }
```

count()

```
int count( void )
```

count() counts the number of children for the element invoked.

Tips

Requires PHP 5.3.0 or higher.

Example

```
$nodeCount = $XMLroot->count();
for ($i = 0; $i < $nodeCount; $i++) { }
```

getDocNamespaces()

```
array getDocNamespaces([ bool $recursive = false
    [, bool $from_root = true ]] )
```

Returns namespaces declared in the XML document.

Tips

- Unlike getNamespaces(), this returns namespaces declared in the document, whether or not they are used.
- By default, getDocNamespaces() only returns namespaces declared in the root node. If $recursive is set to true, it will also return namespaces declared in the child nodes.

Example

```
$namespaces = $XMLroot->getDocNamespaces();
```

getName()

```
string getName( void )
```

Returns the name of the XML element.

Example

```
$name = $randomXMLnode->getName();
```

getNamespaces()

```
array getNamespaces([ bool $recursive = false ] )
```

Returns namespaces used in the XML document.

Tips

- Unlike getDocNamespaces(), this method returns only those namespaces actually used in the document.
- By default, getNamespaces() only returns namespaces declared in the root node. If $recursive is set to true, it will also return namespaces declared in the child nodes.

Example

```
$namespaces = $XMLroot->getNamespaces();
```

registerXPathNamespace()

```
Bool registerXPathNamespace( string $prefix, string $ns )
```

Creates a prefix/namespace context for the next XPath query.
registerXPathNamespace() will create a prefix for the associated namespace,
allowing you to access nodes in that namespace without the need to change code.

Tips

This is helpful if the provider of the XML document alters the namespace prefixes mid-document.

Example

```
$childNode-> registerXPathNamespace (
    'ex', 'http://www.example.com/ex'
);
```

__toString(void)

```
public string __toString ( void )
```

Returns the text content that is directly in the SimpleXMLElement.

Tips

This is helpful for easily getting a string representation.

Example

```
echo $myXMLnode;
```

saveXML()

```
mixed saveXML( string $path )
```

This method is an alias of asXML().

xpath()

```
array xpath( string $path )
```

xpath() searches a SimpleXML node for children matching the XPath query.

Example

```
$nodes = $XMLroot->xpath('/item');
```

Procedural Functions

These are the only functions in the SimpleXML library, and each of them is used for creating a SimpleXMLElement object. There are no procedures for manipulating XML directly, without an object.

simplexml_import_dom()

```
SimpleXMLElement simplexml_import_dom( DOMNode $node
    [, string $class_name = "SimpleXMLElement" ] )
```

As the name suggests, this function takes an object from the DOM library representing an XML node and converts it into a SimpleXML representation of the node so you can use SimpleXML methods.

Example

```
$mySimpleXML = simplexml_import_dom($myDOM);
```

simplexml_load_file()

```
object simplexml_load_file ( string $filename
    [, string $class_name = "SimpleXMLElement"
    [, int $options = 0 [, string $ns = ""
    [, bool $is_prefix = false ]]]] )
```

This is a procedural approach to converting a well-formed XML document into a SimpleXMLElement object. You could also load a file using the SimpleXMLElement constructor. See __construct( ), above.

Tips

- $options requires PHP 5.1.0 or later and Libxml 2.6.0 or later
- Libxml 2 unescapes the $ns URI, so prior to PHP 5.1.0, you have to call rawurlencode( ) first. PHP 5.1.0 and later escapes it automatically.

Example

```
$mySimpleXML = simplexml_load_file(
    '/path/to/example/file.xml'
);
```

simplexml_load_string()

```
object simplexml_load_string( string $data
    [, string $class_name = "SimpleXMLElement"
    [, int $options = 0 [, string $ns = ""
    [, bool $is_prefix = false ]]]] )
```

Takes a well-formed XML string, usually in a variable, and returns it as a SimpleXMLElement object.

Tips

- $options requires PHP 5.1.0 or later and Libxml 2.6.0 or later
- Libxml 2 unescapes the $ns URI, so prior to PHP 5.1.0, you have to call rawurlencode( ) first. PHP 5.1.0 and later escapes it automatically.

Example

```
$XMLfile = fread($fileHandle);
$mySimpleXML = simplexml_load_string($XMLfile);
```

Appendix
B

DOM Function Reference

Method signatures come from the PHP online manual at *http://php.net/dom*, but I have attempted to test each function and to fill in the gaps when the PHP online manual is incomplete or ambiguous. Note that this reference omits properties and methods that have been deprecated or that have been defined but not yet implemented. Please refer to the online manual for the most complete and up-to-date information.

DOM requires both itself and libxml to be enabled. Both of these are enabled by default.

DOMAttr Class

See DOMNode below for methods the DOMAttr class inherits.

Properties

Property	Description
public readonly string $name;	The name of the attribute.
public readonly DOMElement $ownerElement;	The element which contains the attribute.
public string $value;	The value of the attribute

Methods

__construct()

```
DOMAttr __construct( string $name [, string $value ] )
```

__construct( ) creates a new DOMAttr object. It is invoked with the new operator.

Example

```
$myAttr = new DOMAttr('someName', 'someValue');
```

isId()

```
Boolean isId(void)
```

isId( ) checks if an attribute is a defined ID.

Tips

According to the DOM standard, this requires a DTD that defines the attribute ID to be of type ID. You should validate your document before calling isID( ).

Example

```
if (myAttr->isID()) { }
```

DOMCdataSection Class

See DOMText below for methods the DOMCdataSection class inherits.

Methods

__construct()

```
DOMCdataSection __construct( string $value );
```

__construct() creates a new DOMCdataSection object. It is invoked with the new operator.

Tips

This will produce an empty CDATA node if no $value is specified.

Example

```
$myCDATA = new DOMCdataSection('Four score and seven years
ago...');
```

DOMCharacterData Class

See DOMNode below for methods the DOMCharacterData class inherits. Note this class is not intended to be used directly; rather, several classes extend it.

Properties

Property	Description
public string $data;	The contents of the node.
readonly public int $length;	The length of the content, in number of characters.

Methods

appendData()

```
void appendData( string $data )
```

Adds the string $data to the end of the existing DOMCharacterData node's text.

Example

```
$myComment->appendData("$timestamp ...another comment\n");
```

deleteData()

```
void deleteData( int $offset , int $count )
```

Deletes $count number of characters starting at $offset.

Example

```
$myComment->deleteData(0, 24);
```

insertData()

```
void insertData( int $offset , string $data )
```

Inserts $data starting at $offset

Example

```
$myComment->insertData(0,   "2011-01-02...");
```

replaceData()

```
void replaceData( int $offset , int $count ,
    string $data )
```

Replace $count characters starting at $offset with $data.

Example

```
$myComment->replaceData(0, 24, "2011-01-02...");
```

substringData()

```
string substringData( int $offset , int $count )
```

Returns the specified substring.

Example

```
$comment = $myComment->substringData(0, 24);
```

DOMComment Class

See *DOMCharacterData* *above for methods the* *DOMComment* *class inherits.*

Methods

__construct()

```
DOMComment __construct([ string $value ] )
```

__construct() creates a new DOMComment object. It is invoked with the new operator.

Tips

This will produce an empty comment node if no $value is specified. See
DOMDocument::createComment() for a more flexible way to create comment nodes.

Example

```
$myComment = new DOMComment('Copyright 1999');
```

DOMDocument Class

See DOMNode below for methods the DomDocument class inherits.

Properties

Property	Description
readonly public DOMDocumentType $doctype;	The Document Type Declaration associated with this document.
readonly public DOMElement $documentElement;	This is a convenience attribute that allows direct access to the child node that is the document element of the document.
public string $documentURI;	The location of the document or NULL if undefined.
public string $encoding;	Encoding of the document, as specified by the XML declaration. This attribute is not present in the final DOM Level 3 specification, but is the only way of manipulating XML document encoding in this implementation.
public bool $formatOutput;	Nicely formats output with indentations and extra space.
readonly public DOMImplementation $implementation;	The DOMImplementation object that handles this document.
public bool $preserveWhiteSpace = true;	Do not remove redundant white space. Defaults to TRUE.
public bool $recover;	Enables recovery mode, i.e. trying to parse non-well formed documents. *NOTE: This attribute is not part of the DOM specification and is specific to libxml.*
public bool $resolveExternals;	Set it to TRUE to load external entities from a DOCTYPE declaration. This is useful for including character entities in your XML document.
public bool $strictErrorChecking = true;	Throw DOMException on errors. Defaults to TRUE.

Property	Description
`public bool $substituteEntities;`	Whether or not to substitute entities. *NOTE: This attribute is not part of the DOM specification and is specific to libxml.*
`public bool $validateOnParse = false;`	Validates against the DTD as it loads. Defaults to FALSE.
`readonly public string $xmlEncoding;`	An attribute specifying, as part of the XML declaration, the encoding of this document. This is NULL when unspecified or when it is not known, such as when the Document was created in memory.
`public bool $xmlStandalone;`	An attribute specifying, as part of the XML declaration, whether this document is standalone. This is FALSE when unspecified.
`public string $xmlVersion;`	An attribute specifying, as part of the XML declaration, the version number of this document. If there is no declaration and if this document supports the "XML" feature, the value is "1.0".

Methods

__construct()

```
DOMDocument __construct([string $version
    [, string $encoding]])
```

__construct() creates a new DOMDocument object. It is invoked with the new operator.

Tips

If you load an XML document with version and encoding specified in the < ?xml . . . ?> tag, it will override $version and $encoding.

Example

```
$myDOMdoc = new DOMDocument();
```

createAttribute( )

```
DOMAttr createAttribute(string $name)
```

`createAttribute( )` creates a new instance of class `DOMAttr`. The new node will not show up unless it is inserted into the document.

Example

```
$attrObj = $myDOMdoc->createAttribute('SSN');
$person->appendChild($attrObj);
```

createAttributeNS( )

```
DOMAttr createAttributeNS( string $namespaceURI ,
    string $qualifiedName )
```

This method creates a new `DOMAttr` object. The new node will not show up unless it is inserted into the document

Example

```
$newNS = $myDOMdoc->createAttributeNS(
    'http://www.example.com/ex',
    'EX:example'
);
$myNode->appendChild($newNS);
```

createCDATASection( )

```
DOMCDATASection createCDATASection( string $data )
```

This method creates a new instance of the `DOMCDATASection` class. The new node will not show up unless it is inserted into the document.

Example

```
$charNode = $myDOMdoc->createCDATASection(
    'Lots of text goes here'
);
$myNode->appendChild($charNode);
```

createComment()

```
DOMComment createComment( string $data )
```

This method creates a new instance of the DOMComment class. The new node will not show up unless it is inserted into the document.

Example

```
$commentNode = $myDOMdoc->createComment('Comment here');
$myNode->appendChild($commentNode);
```

createDocumentFragment()

```
DOMDocumentFragment createDocumentFragment( void )
```

This method creates a new DOMDocumentFragment object. The new node will not show up unless it is inserted into the document.

Tips

DOMDocumentFragments are useful for concatenating multiple XML documents or processing character entities differently than a DOMDocument.

Example

```
$docFrag = $myDOMdoc->createDocumentFragment();
$docFrag->appendXML($xmlString);
$myNode->documentElement->appendChild($docFrag);
```

createElement()

```
DOMElement createElement(string $name [, string $value ])
```

This method creates a DOMElement object. The new node will not show up unless it is inserted into the document.

Example

```
$myElement = $myDOMdoc->createElement('person');
$myNode->appendChild($myElement);
```

createElementNS()

```
DOMElement createElementNS(string $namespaceURI ,
    string $qualifiedName [, string $value ])
```

This method creates a new element node with an associated namespace. The new node will not show up unless it is inserted into the document.

Example

```
$myElement = $myDOMdoc->createElementNS(
    'http://www.example.com/ex', 'EX:example', 'exValue'
);
$myNode->appendChild($myElement);
```

createEntityReference()

```
DOMEntityReference createEntityReference( string $name )
```

This method creates a new DOMEntityReference object—that is, a special character like   or <. The new object will not show up unless it is inserted into the document.

Example

```
$myEntity = $myDOMdoc->createEntityReference('nbsp');
$myNode->appendChild($myEntity);
```

createProcessingInstruction()

```
DOMProcessingInstruction createProcessingInstruction(
    string $target [, string $data ] )
```

This method creates a new DOMProcessingInstruction object. The new node will not show up unless it is inserted into the document. See the discussion on processing instructions in *Chapter 6, Advanced DOM*.

Example

```
$myProcInstr = $myDOMdoc->createProcessingInstruction(
    'php', 'echo "Hello World";'
);
$myDOMdoc->appendChild($myProcInstr);
```

createTextNode()

```
DOMText createTextNode( string $content )
```

This method creates a new DOMText object. The new node will not show up unless it is inserted into the document.

Example

```
$myText = $myDOMdoc->createTextNode('Some text');
$myNode->appendChild($myText);
```

getElementById()

```
DOMElement getElementById( string $elementId )
```

getElementById() is similar to getElementsByTagName() (below) but searches for a specific element with a given ID.

Tips

For this method to work, you either need to set some ID attributes with setIdAttribute() or a Document Type Definition (DTD) which defines an attribute to be of type ID. In the case of a DTD, you will need to validate your document with DOMDocument::validate() or by setting DOMDocument's validateOnParse property to TRUE before using this method.

Example

```
$myElement = $myDOMdoc->getElementById('Record8');
```

getElementsByTagName()

```
DOMNodeList getElementsByTagName( string $name )
```

getElementsByTagName() returns a new DOMNodeList object containing the elements with a given tag name.

Example

```
$myDOMlist = $myDOMdoc->getElementsByTagName('employee');
for ($i=0; $i<$myDOMlist->length; $i++) {
    $myDOMlist->$item($i);
}
```

getElementsByTagNameNS( )

```
DOMNodeList getElementsByTagNameNS( string $namespaceURI,
    string $localName )
```

Returns a DOMNodeList object of all elements with a given local name and namespace URI.

Example

```
$myDOMlist = $myDOMdoc->getElementsByTagNameNS(
    'http://www.example.com/ex', '*'
);
for ($i=0; $i<$myDOMlist->length; $i++) {$myDOMlist->$item($i);}
```

importNode( )

```
DOMNode importNode( DOMNode $importedNode [, bool $deep ] )
```

Associates a copy of a given DOMNode object with the current DOMDocument.

Tips

To copy $importedNode's attributes, $deep needs to be set to TRUE.

Example

```
$importedNode = $myDOMdoc->importNode(
    $foreignNode, TRUE
);
$myDOMdoc->appendChild($importedNode);
```

load( )

```
mixed load( string $filename [, int $options = 0 ] )
```

Loads an XML document from a file.

Tips

Unix-style paths with forward slashes can cause significant performance degradation on Windows systems. Use realpath( ) to convert the pathname in such a case.

Example

```
$newDOMdoc = DOMDocument::load(
    '/path/to/file', LIBXML_NOBLANKS
);
```

loadHTML()

```
bool loadHTML ( string $source [, int $options = 0 ] )
```

The method parses the HTML contained in the string $source. Unlike XML, HTML does not have to be well-formed to load.

Tips

$options was added in PHP 5.4.0 to specify additional Libxml parameters.

Example

```
$myWebPage = file_get_contents('http://www.example.com');
$myDOMdoc->loadHTML($myWebPage);
```

loadHTMLFile()

```
bool loadHTMLFile( string $filename [, int $options = 0 ] )
```

The method parses the HTML document in $filepath. Unlike XML, HTML does not have to be well-formed to load.

Tips

$options was added in PHP 5.4.0 to specify additional Libxml parameters.

Example

```
$myDOMdoc = new DOMDocument();
$myDOMdoc->loadHTMLFile('/path/to/file.html');
```

loadXML()

```
mixed loadXML(string $source [, int $options = 0 ])
```

Loads an XML document from a string.

Tips

$options was added in PHP 5.4.0 to specify additional Libxml parameters.

Example

```
$XMLdata = fread($filehandle);
$myDOMdoc->loadXML($XMLdata);
```

normalizeDocument()

```
void normalizeDocument( void )
```

This method acts as if you saved and then loaded the document, putting the document in "normal" form. See also normalize( ) under DOMNode.

Example

```
$myDOMdoc->normalizeDocument( )
```

registerNodeClass()

```
bool registerNodeClass( string $baseclass ,
    string $extendedclass )
```

This method allows you to register your own extended DOM class to be used by the PHP DOM extension.

Tips

This method is not part of the DOM standard.

Example

```
$myDOMdoc->registerNodeClass(
    'DOMElement', 'mySpecializedElement'
);
```

relaxNGValidate()

```
bool relaxNGValidate( string $filename )
```

Performs RELAX NG (RNG) validation on the document based on the given RNG schema file. See *http://www.relaxng.org* for more information.

Example

```
$myDOMdoc->relaxNGValidate('/path/to/RNG/file');
```

relaxNGValidateSource()

```
bool relaxNGValidateSource( string $source )
```

Performs RELAX NG (RNG) validation on the document based on the given RNG schema string. See *http://www.relaxng.org* for more information.

Example

```
$myDOMdoc->relaxNGValidateSource($myRNGschema);
```

save()

```
int save ( string $filename [, int $options ] )
```

Creates an XML document from the DOM representation. This method is usually called after building a new DOM document from scratch.

Tips

$options was added in PHP 5.1.0 to specify Libxml options but only LIBXML_NOEMPTYTAG is supported.

Example

```
$myDOMdoc->save('/path/to/save/file');
```

saveHTML()

```
string saveHTML([ DOMNode $node = NULL ] )
```

Creates an HTML document from a DOMNode object. This method is usually called after building a new DOM document from scratch.

Tips

$node was added in PHP 5.3.6

Example

```
$someHTML = $myDOMdoc->saveHTML();
```

saveHTMLFile()

```
int saveHTMLFile( string $filename )
```

Creates an HTML document from the DOM representation. This method is usually called after building a new DOM document from scratch.

Example

```
$myDOMdoc->saveHTMLFile('/path/to/save/file');
```

saveXML()

```
string saveXML([ DOMNode $node [, int $options ]] )
```

Creates an XML document string from the DOM representation.

Tips

$options was added in 5.1.0 to specify Libxml options but only LIBXML_NOEMPTYTAG is supported.

Example

```
echo $myDOMdoc->saveXML();
```

schemaValidate()

```
bool schemaValidate( string $filename [, int $flags ] )
```

Validates a document based on an XML schema defined in the given file.

Tips

$flags is a bitmask of Libxml schema validation flags. Available since PHP 5.5.2, only LIBXML_SCHEMA_CREATE is supported.

Example

```
$myDOMdoc->schemaValidate ('/path/to/XML/schema);
```

schemaValidateSource()

```
bool schemaValidateSource( string $source [, int $flags ] )
```

Validates a document based on a schema defined in the given string.

Tips

$flags is a bitmask of Libxml schema validation flags. Available since PHP 5.5.2, only LIBXML_SCHEMA_CREATE is supported.

Example

```
$myDOMdoc->schemaValidateSource($myXMLschema);
```

validate()

```
bool validate( void )
```

Validates the document based on its Document Type Definition (DTD).

Tips

- If the document has no DTD, this method will return FALSE.
- You can also set the validateOnParse property of DOMDocument to TRUE to make a DTD validation.
- See also the W3C's validator at *http://validator.w3.org*.

Example

```
$myDOMdoc->validate();
```

xinclude()

```
int DomDocument->xinclude([$options])
```

This method substitutes XIncludes in a DomDocument object.

Tips

- Due to libxml2 automatically resolving entities, this method will produce unexpected results if the included XML file has an attached DTD.
- $options was added in PHP 5.1.0. to spicify Libxml parameters.
- See *http://www.w3.org/TR/xinclude/* for more information.

Example

```
$myDOMdoc->xinclude(LIBXML_NOENT);
```

DOMDocumentFragment Class

See DOMNode *below for methods the* DOMDocument *class inherits.*

Methods

appendXML(string $data)

```
Boolean appendXML($data)
```

Appends $data to an existing XML document.

Tips

This is a convenience function that is not part of the DOM standard.

Example

```
$docFrag = $DOMdoc->createDocumentFragment();
$docFrag->appendXML('<node>value</node>');
```

DOMDocumentType Class

See DOMNode below for methods the DOMDocument class inherits.

The DOMDocumentType class is an object representation of the XML document's DOCTYPE declaration. It declares no methods—only properties.

Properties

Property	Description
readonly public string $DOMDocumentType->publicId;	The public identifier of the external subset.
readonly public string $systemId;	The system identifier of the external subset. This may be an absolute URI or not.
readonly public string $name;	The name of DTD; i.e., the name immediately following the DOCTYPE keyword.
readonly public DOMNamedNodeMap $entities;	A DOMNamedNodeMap object containing the general entities, both external and internal, declared in the DTD.
readonly public DOMNamedNodeMap $notations;	A DOMNamedNodeMap containing the notations declared in the DTD.
readonly public string $internalSubset;	The internal subset as a string, or null if there is none. This is does not contain the delimiting square brackets.

DOMElement Class

See *DOMNode below for methods the DOMElement class inherits.*

Properties

Property	Description
readonly public string $tagName;	The element's tag name.
readonly public bool $schemaTypeInfo ;	The element name

Methods

__construct

```
public __construct ( string $name [, string $value
    [, string $namespaceURI ]] )
```

_construct create a new read-only DOMElement object.

getAttribute()

```
string getAttribute( string $name )
```

Retrieves the value of the attribute called $name from the current node.

Example

```
$empID = $employeeElement->getAttribute('EmployeeID');
```

getAttributeNode()

```
DOMAttr getAttributeNode( string $name )
```

Returns a DOMAttr object representing $name.

Example

```
$myAttr = $employeeElement->getAttributeNode('empID');
```

getAttributeNodeNS()

```
DOMAttr getAttributeNodeNS( string $namespaceURI ,
    string $localName )
```

Effectively a namespace-qualified version of getAttributeNode(). Returns the attribute node in the namespace identified by $namespaceURI and with the local name $localName for the current node.

Example

```
$myAttr = $employeeElt>getAttributeNodeNS(
    'http://ns.adobe.com/mxml/2009', 'empID'
);
```

getAttributeNS()

```
string getAttributeNS( string $namespaceURI ,
    string $localName )
```

Effectively a namespace-qualified version of getAttribute(). Retrieves the value of the attribute in namespace $namespaceURI with the local name $localName for the current node.

Example

```
$empID = $employeeElt->getAttributeNS(
    'http://ns.adobe.com/mxml/2009', 'EmployeeID'
);
```

getElementsByTagName()

```
DOMNodeList getElementsByTagName( string $name )
```

This method returns a DOMNodeList object of all descendant elements with a given tag name,

Tips

Elements are returned in the order in which they are encountered.

Example

```
$allBookNodes = $DOMdoc->getElementsByTagName('book');
```

getElementsByTagNameNS()

```
DOMNodeList getElementsByTagNameNS( string $namespaceURI ,
string $localName )
```

This method returns a DOMNodeList object of all descendant elements with a given tag name within the namespace defined by $namespaceURI. It's effectively a namespace-qualified version of getElementsByTagName( )

Tips

Elements are returned in the order in which they are encountered.

Example

```
$allBookNodes = $DOMdoc->getElementsByTagNameNS(
    'http://ns.adobe.com/mxml/2009', 'book'
);
```

hasAttribute()

```
bool hasAttribute( string $name )
```

Indicates whether the element contains an attribute named $name.

Example

```
if ($myNode->hasAttribute('ISBN')) { }
```

hasAttributeNS()

```
bool hasAttributeNS( string $namespaceURI ,
    string $localName )
```

Indicates whether the element has a member attribute in namespace $namespaceURI named $localName. Effectively a namespace-qualified version of hasAttribute( ).

Example

```
if ($myNode->hasAttribute('http://ns.adobe.com/mxml/2009', 'ISBN'))
{ }
```

removeAttribute()

```
bool removeAttribute( string $name )
```

Removes attribute named $name from the called element.

Example

```
$myDOMelement->removeAttribute('EmployeeID');
```

removeAttributeNode()

```
bool removeAttributeNode( DOMAttr $oldnode )
```

Removes attribute object $oldnode from the element.

Example

```
$bookNode->removeAttributeNode(
    $bookNode->getAttributeNode('ISBN')
);
```

removeAttributeNS()

```
bool removeAttributeNS ( string $namespaceURI ,
    string $localName )
```

Removes an attribute in namespace $namespaceURI called $localName from the element. A namespace-qualified version of removeAttribute().

Example

```
$myDOMelement->removeAttribute(
    'http://ns.adobe.com/mxml/2009', 'EmployeeID'
);
```

setAttribute()

```
DOMAttr setAttribute( string $name , string $value )
```

Sets an attribute named $name to $value on the called element. If the attribute does not exist, it will be created.

Example

```
$bookNode->setAttribute('ISBN', 'NA');
```

setAttributeNode()

```
DOMAttr setAttributeNode ( DOMAttr $attr )
```

Adds a new attribute node to the called element.

Example

```
$myAttr = new DOMAttr('foo', 'bar');
$myElement->setAttributeNode($myAttr);
```

setAttributeNodeNS()

```
DOMAttr setAttributeNodeNS( DOMAttr $attr )
```

Adds new attribute object node to an element.

Tips

setAttributeNodeNS will first check if the attribute with the same name and in the same namespace as $attr already exists before replacing it with the new attribute.

Example

```
$myAttr = new DOMAttr('s:foo', 'bar');
$myElement->setAttributeNodeNS($myAttr);
```

setAttributeNS()

```
void setAttributeNS( string $namespaceURI ,
    string $qualifiedName , string $value )
```

Sets an attribute with namespace $namespaceURI and name $name to $value on the called element object. If the attribute does not exist, it will be created. Effectively a namespace-qualified version of setAttribute().

Example

```
$bookNode->setAttributeNS(
    'http://ns.adobe.com/mxml/2009', 'ISBN', 'NA'
);
```

setIdAttribute()

```
void setIdAttribute( string $name , bool $isId )
```

Declares the attribute $name to be of type ID. See the discussion of ID types in _Chapter 6, Advanced DOM_.

Example

```
$myElement->setIdAttribute('id', true);
```

setIdAttributeNode()

```
void setIdAttributeNode( DOMAttr $attr , bool $isId )
```

Declares the DOMAttr object $attr to be of type ID. See the discussion of ID types in _Chapter 6, Advanced DOM_.

Example

```
$myAttr = new DOMAttr('id', 1);
$myElement->setIdAttribute($myAttr, true);
```

setIdAttributeNS()

```
void setIdAttributeNS ( string $namespaceURI ,
    string $localName , bool $isId )
```

Declares the attribute $localName with namespace $namespaceURI to be of type ID.

Example

```
$myElement->setIdAttribute(
    'http://ns.adobe.com/mxml/2009', 'id', true
);
```

DOMEntity Class

See DOMNode *below for methods the* DOMEntity *class inherits.*

DOMEntity declares no methods of its own—only properties.

Properties

Property	Description
readonly public string $publicId;	The public identifier associated with the entity if specified, and NULL otherwise.
readonly public string $systemId;	The system identifier associated with the entity if specified, and NULL otherwise. This may be an absolute URI or not.
readonly public string $notationName;	For unparsed entities, the name of the notation for the entity. For parsed entities, this is NULL.
public string $actualEncoding;	An attribute specifying the encoding used for this entity at the time of parsing, when it is an external parsed entity. This is NULL if it an entity from the internal subset or if it is not known.
readonly public string $encoding;	An attribute specifying, as part of the text declaration, the encoding of this entity, when it is an external parsed entity. This is NULL otherwise.
readonly public string $version;	An attribute specifying, as part of the text declaration, the version number of this entity, when it is an external parsed entity. This is NULL otherwise.

DOMEntityReference Class

See *DOMNode* below for methods the *DOMEntity* class inherits.

Methods

__construct()

```
DOMEntityReference __construct( string $name )
```

__construct() creates a new DOMEntityReference object, which can be used to insert special characters into the DOM document.

Example

```
$space = new DOMEntityReference('nbsp');
$myDOMnode->appendChild($space);
```

DOMException Class

DOMException is a simple, DOM-specific implementation of the Exception class. It defines one custom property.

Properties

Property	Description
readonly public int $code;	An integer indicating the type of error generated

DOMImplementation Class

The DOMImplementation class provides a number of methods for performing operations that are independent of any particular instance of the document object model. You can retrieve a DOMImplementation object from the $implementation property of a DOMDocument object.

Methods

__construct()

```
DOMImplementation __construct( void )
```

Creates a new DOMImplemenation object.

Example

```
$myDOMimp = new DOMImplementation();
```

createDocument()

```
DOMDocument createDocument ([ string $namespaceURI = NULL
    [, string $qualifiedName = NULL
    [, DOMDocumentType $doctype = NULL ]]] )
```

createDocument creates a new DOMDocument object of the specified type with its document element.

Tips

createDocument() may be used to create new DOMDocument objects.

Example

```
$myDOMimp = new DOMImplementation();
$DOMdoc = $myDOMimp ->createDocument();
```

createDocumentType()

```
DOMDocumentType createDocumentType(
    [ string $qualifiedName = NULL
    [, string $publicId = NULL
    [, string $systemId = NULL ]]] )
```

createDocumentType will create an empty DOMDocumentType object.

Example

```
$myDOMimp = new DOMImplementation();
$docType = $myDOMnode->createDocumentType();
```

hasFeature()

```
Boolean hasFeature( string $feature , string $version )
```

hasFeature will test if the DOM implementation implements a specific feature, like "HTML" or "CSS2".

Tips

You can find a list of all features at
http://www.w3.org/TR/2000/REC-DOM-Level-2-Core-20001113/
introduction.html#ID-Conformance

Example

```
$myDOMimp = new DOMImplementation();
if ($myDOMimp->hasFeature('Core', '2.0')) { }
```

DOMNamedNodeMap Class

You can not construct a DOMNamedNodeMap manually, but it is returned by a handful of other classes.

Properties

Property	Description
`readonly public int $length;`	The number of nodes in the map. Valid range is 0 to $length–1.

Methods

getNamedItem()

```
DOMNode getNamedItem( string $name )
```

getNamedItem() retrieves the node specified by $name.

Example

```
foreach ($myNodeList as $node) {
    echo $node->attributes
            ->getNamedItem('id') . "\n";
}
```

getNamedItemNS()

```
DOMNode getNamedItemNS( string $namespaceURI ,
    string $localName )
```

A complement to getNamedItem(), getNamedItemNS() retrieves the node specified by $namespaceURI and $localName.

Example

```
foreach ($myNodeList as $node) {
    echo $node->attributes
            ->getNamedItemNS(
                'http://ns.adobe.com/mxml/2009', 'Script'
            )->nodeValue . "\n";
}
```

item()

```
DOMNode item( int $index )
```

item() retrieves the node specified by $index.

Example

```php
$myNodeMap = $myDOMElement->attributes;
for ($i=0; $i<$myNodeMap->length; $i++) {
    echo $myNodeMap->item($i)->nodeValue . "\n";
}
```

DOMNode Class

Both the DOMDocument and DOMElement classes extend the DOMNode class, so these methods are available to objects of both types except as noted. Note that references to DOMNode objects below could refer to any of its child classes as well.

Properties

Property	Description
public readonly string $DOMNode->nodeName;	Returns the most accurate name for the current node type
public string $nodeValue;	The value of this node, depending on its type
public readonly int $nodeType;	Gets the type of the node. See http://php.net/dom.constants for valid types.
public readonly DOMNode $parentNode;	The parent of this node
public readonly DOMNodeList $childNodes;	A DOMNodeList that contains all children of this node. If there are no children, the DOMNodeList is empty.
public readonly DOMNode $firstChild;	The first child of this node. If there is no such node, this returns NULL.
public readonly DOMNode $lastChild;	The last child of this node. If there is no such node, this returns NULL.
public readonly DOMNode $previousSibling;	The node immediately preceding this node. If there is no such node, this returns NULL.
public readonly DOMNode $nextSibling;	The node immediately following this node. If there is no such node, this returns NULL.
public readonly DOMNamedNodeMap $attributes;	A DOMNamedNodeMap containing the attributes of this node (if it is a DOMElement) or NULL otherwise.
public readonly DOMDocument $ownerDocument;	The DOMDocument object associated with this node.
public readonly string $namespaceURI;	The namespace URI of this node, or NULL if it is unspecified.

Property	Description
`public string $prefix;`	The namespace prefix of this node, or `NULL` if it is unspecified.
`public readonly string $localName;`	Returns the local part of the qualified name of this node.
`public readonly string $baseURI;`	The absolute base URI of this node or `NULL` if the implementation wasn't able to obtain an absolute URI.
`public string $textContent;`	This attribute returns the text content of this node and its descendants.

Methods

appendChild()

```
DOMNode appendChild( DOMNode $newnode )
```

appendChild() adds a child to an existing list of DOM children or creates a new list of children.

Example

```
$DOMdoc = new DOMDocument();
$node = $DOMdoc->createElement('paragraph');
$newnode = $DOMdoc->appendChild($node);
```

C14N()

```
public string C14N ([ bool $exclusive
    [, bool $with_comments [, array $xpath
    [, array $ns_prefixes ]]]] )
```

C14N() canonicalizes nodes to a string. Canonicalization lets you normalize features of an XML document such that you can compare it with other forms of the XML data.

C14NFile()

```
public int C14NFile ( string $uri [, bool $exclusive
    [, bool $with_comments [, array $xpath
    [, array $ns_prefixes ]]]] )
```

C14NFile() canonicalizes nodes to a file. Canonicalization lets you normalize features of an XML document such that you can compare it with other forms of the XML data.

cloneNode()

```
DOMNode cloneNode([ bool $deep ] )
```

Creates a copy of the node on which cloneNode() is called.

Example

```
$duplicateNode = $myXMLnode->cloneNode();
```

getLineNo()

```
int getLineNo( void )
```

Returns the line number indicating where the node was first defined.

Tips

Results can vary depending on the platform on which you created your document and how it is formatted. This method should be taken as a general guideline rather than an exact position.

Example

```
$lineNum = $myXMLnode->getElementsByTagName('paragraph')
                      ->getLineNo();
```

getNodePath()

```
public string getNodePath ( void )
```

getNodePath returns an Xpath for a node.

hasAttributes()

```
bool hasAttributes( void )
```

hasAttributes() just checks if the node has any attributes. Note that the tested node must be a DOMElement or another node of type XML_ELEMENT_NODE.

Example

```
if ($myXMLnode->hasAttributes()) { }
```

hasChildNodes()

```
bool hasChildNodes( void )
```

hasChildNodes() checks if the node has any children.

Example

```
if ($myXMLnode->hasChildNodes()) { }
```

insertBefore()

```
DOMNode insertBefore( DOMNode $newnode
     [, DOMNode $refnode ] )
```

A counterpart to appendChild(), this method inserts $newnode right before the $refnode. If you plan to do further modifications on the appended child you must access it through the returned reference node.

Tips

If you are accessing a text node, you will have to access the $parentNode property (i.e. the tag) for this method to work as expected.

Example

```
$person1 = $xpathObj->query('/contacts/person')->item(0);
$john = $DOMobj->createElement('person', 'John');
$person1->parentNode->insertBefore($john, $person1);
```

isDefaultNamespace()

```
bool isDefaultNamespace( string $namespaceURI )
```

Tells you whether $namespaceURI is the default namespace.

Example

```
$ns = 'http://www.example.com/ex'
if ($myNode->isDefaultNamespace($ns)) {
    // do something
}
```

isSameNode()

```
bool isSameNode( DOMNode $node )
```

This method indicates if two variables reference the same node. The comparison is based on reference address, not content.

Example

```
$yourNode = $myNode;
if ($myNode->isSameNode($yourNode)) { }
```

isSupported()

```
bool isSupported( string $feature , string $version )
```

Checks if a specific feature is supported for the specified version.

Tips

Example features: 'Core', 'XML'. A comprehensive list can be found in the W3C's DOM specification under the "Conformance" section at *http://www.w3.org/TR/2000/REC-DOM-Level-2-Core-20001113/introduction.html#ID-Conformance*

Example

```
if ($myXMLnode->isSupported('Core', '2.0')) { }
```

lookupNamespaceURI()

```
string lookupNamespaceURI( string $prefix )
```

Returns a namespace URI of the node based on $prefix.

Example

```
$URL = $myXMLnode->lookupNamespaceURI('pre');
if ($myXMLnode->isDefaultNamespace($URL)) {
    // do something
}
```

lookupPrefix()

```
string lookupPrefix( string $namespaceURI )
```

The counterpart to lookupNamespaceURI(), lookupPrefix() returns the namespace prefix of the node based on a given namespace URI.

Example

```
$pre = $myXMLnode->lookupPrefix('http://www.example.com/ex');
```

normalize()

```
void normalize( void )
```

Normalizes the node. See the discussion on Normalization in *Chapter 6, Advanced DOM*.

Tips

This is effectively equivalent to saving and then reloading the document. See also normalizeDocument() under the DOMDocument section.

Example

```
$myXMLnode->normalize();
```

removeChild()

```
DOMNode removeChild( DOMNode $oldnode )
```

Removes the specified child from a list of children.

Tips

This method should be called on the parent node of the child list you want to modify. The easiest approach is to access the parentNode property of $oldnode.

Example

```
$childToRemove = $xpath->query('/contacts/person[.="John"]')
                        ->item(0);
$removedChild = $myXMLnode->removeChild($childToRemove);
```

replaceChild()

```
DOMNode replaceChild( DOMNode $newnode , DOMNode $oldnode )
```

This method replaces the existing child $oldnode with the DOMNode object $newnode. If $newnode is already a child it will not be added a second time.

Tips

Like removeChild( ), this method should be called on the parent node of the child list you want to modify. The easiest approach is to access the parentNode property of $oldnode.

Example

```
$Jon = $xpath->query('/contacts/person[.="Jon"]')->item(0);
$Sue = $xpath->query('/employees/person[.="Sue"]')->item(0);
$parent = $Sue->parentNode;
$parent->replaceChild($Jon, $Sue);
```

DOMNodeList Class

DOMNodeLists act like traversable arrays of DOMNodes, and are frequently what you receive from an XPath query. You can traverse a DOMNodeList with foreach().

Properties

Property	Description
readonly public int $length;	The number of nodes in the list, in the range of 0 to $length−1.

Methods

item()

```
DOMNode item( int $index )
```

item() retrieves a specific node from the list, as specified by $index.

Example

```
$myNodeList = $DOMdoc->getElementsByTagName('book');
for ($i=0; $i<$myNodeList->length; $i++) {
    $myNode = $myNodeList->item($i);
}
```

DOMNotation Class

See DOMNode above for methods the DOMNotation class inherits.

DOMNotation declares no methods—only properties.

Properties

Property	Description
readonly public string $publicId;	The public identifier associated with the entity if specified, and NULL otherwise.
readonly public string $systemId;	The system identifier associated with the entity if specified, and NULL otherwise. This may be an absolute URI or not.

DOMProcessingInstruction **Class**

See DOMNode *above for methods the* DOMNotation *class inherits.*

Properties

Property	Description
`readonly public string $target;`	The name of the processing instruction; i.e. the string immediately following <?
`public string $data;`	The contents of the <? ?> tags.

Methods

__construct()

```
DOMProcessingInstruction __construct( string $name
    [, string $value ] )
```

__construct() creates a new DOMProcessingInstruction object, which produces an XML processing instruction between <? ?> delimiters.

Tips

An object of type DOMProcessingInstruction is read-only. For a more flexible method of creating processing instructions, try DOMDocument::createProcessingInstruction().

Example

```
$procI = new DOMProcessingInstruction(
    'php',
    'echo "This is a processing instruction";'
);
```

DOMText Class

See `DOMCharacterData` *above for methods the* `DOMText` *class inherits.*

Properties

Property	Description
`readonly public string $wholeText;`	Holds all the text of adjacent Text nodes–i.e. nodes that are not separated by Element, Comment or Processing Instruction nodes.

Methods

__construct()

```
`DOMText __construct([ string $value ] )`
```

`__construct()` creates a new DOMText object.

Tips

If `$value` is empty, `__construct()` will create an empty node. You can also create a text node with `DOMDocument::createTextNode()`.

Example

```
$textNode = new DOMText('Four score and seven years ago...');
```

isWhitespaceInElementContent()

```
Boolean isWhitespaceInElementContent( void )
```

`isWhitespaceInElementContent()` does just what it says: returns `true` if the element is whitespace. Note the element must contain *only* whitespace for this method to return `true`.

Tips

This determination is made at document load time, so altering the document after loading could cause this method to return an inaccurate result.

Example

```
If ($myTextNode->isWhitespaceInElementContent()) { }
```

splitText()

```
DOMText splitText( int $offset )
```

splitText() splits a DOMText node into two nodes at $offset.

Tips

The text after the offset is appended to the parent node. If there is no parent node, splitText() effectively truncates the node at $offset.

Example

```
$halfText = $myTextNode->splitText(10);
```

DOMXPath Class

Properties

Property	Description
public DOMDocument $document;	The DOMDocument object on which this DOMXPath object was created.

Methods

__construct()

```
DOMXPath __construct( DOMDocument $doc )
```

__construct() creates a new DOMXPath object.

Tips

The DOMXPath object effectively copies $DOMdoc, so it will continue to run queries on the old document even if you load new XML into the $DOMdoc variable.

Example

```
$myXPath = new DOMXPath($myDOMdoc);
$nodeList = $xpath->query('/library/book');
```

evaluate()

```
mixed evaluate( string $expression [, DOMNode $contextnode
    [, bool $registerNodeNS = true ]] )
```

Executes an XPath query and attempts to return a typed result.

Tips

- evaluate() is very fussy and often requires casting the returned variable for proper data typing. See *Chapter 6*.
- $registerNodeNS was added in PHP v5.3.3.

Example

```
$title = $xpath->evaluate('string(/library/book/title)');
```

query()

```
DOMNodeList query( string $expression [, DOMNode $contextnode
    [, bool $registerNodeNS = true ]] )
```

Executes an XPath query.

Tips

$registerNodeNS was added in PHP v5.3.3.

Example

```
$nodeList = $xpath->query('/library/book');
```

registerNamespace()

```
Boolean registerNamespace( string $prefix ,
    string $namespaceURI )
```

registerNamespace() creates a new DOMXPath object.

Example

```
$xpath->registerNamespace(
    's', 'library://ns.adobe.com/flex/spark'
);
```

registerPHPFunctions()

```
void registerPHPFunctions([ mixed $restrict ] )
```

registerPHPFunctions() allows you to use PHP functions within XPath expressions.

Tips

*   registerPHPFunctions() was added in PHP 5.3.0.
* $restrict is a whitelist of functions. That is, it is a function or functions that
    you want to enable, rather than those you want to exclude.

Example

```
$myXPath->registerPHPFunctions();
$nodeList = $xpath->query(
    '/library/book[php:'
    . 'functionString("substr", title, 0, 3) = "PHP"]'
);
```

Procedural Functions

This is the only procedural function in the DOM library.

dom_import_ simplexml()

```
DOMElement dom_import_simplexml( SimpleXMLElement $node )
```

As the name suggests, this function takes an object from the SimpleXML library representing an XML node and converts it into a DOM representation of the node.

Example

```
$DOMdoc = dom_import_simplexml($mySimpleXML);
```

Appendix C

XMLReader/ XMLWriter Reference

Most of this reference comes from the PHP online manual at *http://php.net/xmlreader* and *http://php.net/xmlwriter*, but I have attempted to test each function and to fill in the gaps when the PHP online manual is incomplete or ambiguous. Note that this reference omits properties and methods that have been deprecated or that have been defined but not yet implemented.

XMLReader and XMLWriter both require libxml to be enabled, which is enabled by default.

XMLReader Class

Constants

Constant	Usage
const int NONE = 0;	No node.
const int ELEMENT = 1;	Start element.
const int ATTRIBUTE = 2;	Attribute node.
const int TEXT = 3;	Text node.
const int CDATA = 4;	CDATA node.
const int ENTITY_REF = 5;	Entity Reference node.
const int ENTITY = 6;	Entity Declaration node.
const int PI = 7;	Processing Instruction node.
const int COMMENT = 8;	Comment node.
const int DOC = 9;	Document node.
const int DOC_TYPE = 10;	Document Type node.
const int DOC_FRAGMENT = 11;	Document Fragment node.
const int NOTATION = 12;	Notation node.
const int WHITESPACE = 13;	Whitespace node.
const int SIGNIFICANT_WHITESPACE = 14;	Significant Whitespace node.
const int END_ELEMENT = 15;	End Element.
const int END_ENTITY = 16;	End Entity
const int XML_DECLARATION = 17;	XML Declaration node.

XMLReader Parser Options

Constant	Usage
`const int LOADDTD = 1;`	Load DTD, but do not validate.
`const int DEFAULTATTRS = 2;`	Load DTD and default attributes, but do not validate.
`const int VALIDATE = 3;`	Load DTD and validate while parsing.
`const int SUBST_ENTITIES = 4;`	Substitute entities and expand references

Properties

Constant	Usage
`readonly int $attributeCount;`	The number of attributes the node contains
`readonly string $baseURI;`	The base URI of the node
`readonly int $depth;`	Depth of the node in the tree, starting at 0
`readonly bool $hasAttributes;`	Indicates if the node has attributes
`readonly bool $hasValue;`	Indicates if node has a text value
`readonly bool $isDefault;`	Indicates if attribute is default, as defined in the DTD
`readonly bool $isEmptyElement;`	Indicates if node is an empty element tag
`readonly string $localName;`	The local name of the node
`readonly string $name;`	The qualified name of the node
`readonly string $namespaceURI;`	The URI of the namespace associated with the node
`readonly int $nodeType;`	The type of node
`readonly string $prefix;`	The prefix of the namespace associated with the node
`readonly string $value;`	The text value of the node
`readonly string $xmlLang;`	The xml:lang scope which the node resides

Methods

close( )

```
bool close( void )
```

Closes the input the XMLReader object is currently parsing.

Example

```
$XMLreaderDoc->close( );
```

expand( )

```
DOMNode expand( [ DOMNode $basenode ] )
```

Returns a copy of the current node as a DOMNode object.

Example

```
$DOMdoc = $XMLreaderDoc->expand( );
```

getAttribute( )

```
string getAttribute( string $name )
```

Returns the value of a named attribute or NULL.

Example

```
$nodeID = $XMLreaderDoc=>getAttribute('id');
```

getAttributeNo( )

```
string getAttributeNo( int $index)
```

Returns the value of an attribute based on its numerical position or an empty string if the attribute can't be found.

Tips

As with most PHP indexes, getAttributeNo( ) starts counting at zero.

Example

```
$nodeID = $XMLreaderDoc->getAttributeNo(0);
```

getAttributeNs()

```
string getAttributeNs( string $localName ,
    string $namespaceURI )
```

Returns the value of an attribute by name and namespace URI or an empty string if attribute does not exist or is not positioned on an element node.

Tips

Namespaces are more likely to be assigned to tags than attributes, so this has little utility.

Example

```
$nodeID = $XMLreaderDoc->getAttributeNs(
    'id', 'library://ns.adobe.com/flex/mx'
);
```

getParserProperty()

```
bool getParserProperty ( int $property )
```

Indicates whether specified property has been set.

Example

```
if ($XMLreaderDoc->getParserProperty(XMLReader::VALIDATE)
    && $XMLreaderDoc->isValid() ) {
    //...start parsing
}
```

isValid()

```
bool isValid( void )
```

Returns a boolean indicating whether the document being parsed is currently valid.

Tips

You must set XMLReader::VALIDATE to true before calling this method.

Example

```
$XMLreaderDoc = new XMLReader();
$XMLreaderDoc->open('filename.xml');
$XMLreaderDoc->setParserProperty(XMLReader::VALIDATE, true);
if ($XMLreaderDoc->isValid()) {
    // start parsing
}
```

lookupNamespace( )

```
bool lookupNamespace ( string $prefix )
```

Lookup in scope namespace for a given prefix.

Example

```
$namespaceURL = $XMLreaderDoc->lookupNamespace('mx');
```

moveToAttribute( )

```
bool moveToAttribute( string $name )
```

Positions cursor on the named attribute.

Example

```
$XMLreaderDoc->moveToAttribute('id');
```

moveToAttributeNo( )

```
bool moveToAttributeNo ( int $index )
```

Positions cursor on attribute based on its position.

Tips

Similar to getAttributeNo( ), this counts starting with zero and simply moves the cursor to point at the given attribute on the current node.

Example

```
$XMLreaderDoc->moveToAttributeNo(0);
```

moveToAttributeNs( )

```
bool moveToAttributeNs( string $localName ,
    string $namespaceURI )
```

Positions cursor on the named attribute in specified namespace.

Tips

This routine has limited utility because namespaces are more commonly assigned to tags, not attributes.

Example

```
$XMLreaderDoc->moveToAttributeNS(
    'id', 'library://ns.adobe.com/flex/mx'
);
```

moveToElement( )

```
bool moveToElement( void )
```

Moves cursor to the parent Element of current attribute.

Tips

A companion to the moveToAttribute...( ) methods, this "backs the cursor out" to point at the tag enclosing the attribute at which the cursor is currently pointing.

Example

```
$XMLreaderDoc->moveToElement();
```

moveToFirstAttribute( )

```
bool moveToFirstAttribute( void )
```

Moves cursor to the first attribute.

Example

```
$XMLreaderDoc->moveToFirstAttribute();
```

moveToNextAttribute()

```
bool moveToNextAttribute( void )
```

Moves cursor to the next Attribute if positioned on an Attribute or moves to first attribute if positioned on an Element.

Tips

This allows you to step through each attribute in an element, similar to the way read( ) steps through each element.

Example

```
$XMLreaderDoc->moveToNextAttribute();
```

next()

```
bool next([ string $localname ] )
```

Positions cursor on the next node, skipping all subtrees.

Tips

Use with caution, as it skips all child nodes (and grandchildren, great-grandchildren, etc.)

Example

```
$XMLreaderDoc = new XMLReader();
$XMLreaderDoc->open('filename.xml');
$XMLreaderDoc->next();
```

open()

```
bool open( string $URI [, string $encoding
    [, int $options = 0 ]] )
```

Set the URI containing the XML document to be parsed.

Example

```
$XMLreaderDoc = new XMLReader();
$XMLreaderDoc->open(
    'filename.xml', 'utf-8', LIBXML_NOBLANKS
);
```

read( )

```
bool read ( void )
```

Moves cursor to the next node in the document.

Tips

Unlike next( ), touches every element, including empty ones.

Example

```
while ($XMLreaderDoc->read()) {
    echo $XMLreaderDoc->name . ': '
        . $XMLreaderDoc->readInnerXML();
}
```

readInnerXML( )

```
string readInnerXML ( void )
```

Reads the contents of the current node, including child nodes and markup.

Tips

Returns the current node's child tags and contents, without including the tags enclosing the current node.

Example

```
echo $XMLreaderDoc->readInnerXML();
```

readOuterXML( )

```
string readOuterXML( void )
```

Reads the contents of the current node, including the node itself.

Tips

Includes the tags for the current node, in addition to the child tags and contents.

Example

```
echo $XMLreaderDoc->readOuterXML();
```

readString()

```
string readString( void )
```

Reads the contents of the current node as a string.

Tips

Includes only the string data in the node and all its child nodes, with all ‹tags› removed.

Example

```
echo $XMLreaderDoc->readString();
```

setParserProperty()

```
bool setParserProperty( int $property , bool $value )
```

Set parser options. The options must be set after open() or xml() are called and before the first read() call.

Example

```
$XMLreaderDoc = new XMLReader();
$XMLreaderDoc->open('filename.xml');
$XMLreaderDoc->setParserProperty(XMLReader::VALIDATE, true);
if ($XMLreaderDoc->isValid())
    // start parsing
```

setRelaxNGSchema()

```
bool setRelaxNGSchema( string $filename )
```

Set the filename or URI for the RelaxNG Schema to use for validation. Must be called after open() but before the first read().

Example

```
$XMLreaderDoc = new XMLReader();
$XMLreaderDoc->open('library.xml');
$XMLreaderDoc->setRelaxNGSchema('/path/to/schema.xml');
$XMLreaderDoc->read();
```

setRelaxNGSchemaSource()

```
bool setRelaxNGSchemaSource( string $source )
```

Set the data containing a RelaxNG Schema to use for validation. Must be called after open( ) but before the first read( ).

Example

```
$fh = fopen('/path/to/schema.xml', 'r');
$relaxNGdata = fread($fh);
$XMLreaderDoc = new XMLReader();
$XMLreaderDoc->open('library.xml');
$XMLreaderDoc->setRelaxNGSchemaSource($relaxNGdata);
$XMLreaderDoc->read();
```

setSchema()

```
bool setSchema( string $filename )
```

Use an XML Schema Document to validate the document as it is processed. Activation is only possible before the first read( ).

Example

```
$XMLreaderDoc = new XMLReader();
$XMLreaderDoc->open('library.xml');
$XMLreaderDoc->setSchema('/path/to/schema.xml');
$XMLreaderDoc->read();
```

XML()

```
bool xml( string $source [, string $encoding
    [, int $options = 0 ]] )
```

Set the data containing the XML to parse.

Example

```
$fh = fopen('/path/to/XMLfile.xml', 'r');
$xml = fread($fh);
$XMLreaderDoc = new XMLReader();
$XMLreaderDoc->xml($xml);
```

XMLWriter Class

Unlike the other libraries we've covered in this book, XMLWriter provides both a procedural and object-oriented approach to its methods. Object-oriented calls are denoted by XMLWriter::methodName().

Methods

endAttribute()

```
bool XMLWriter::endAttribute( void )

bool xmlwriter_end_attribute( resource $xmlwriter )
```

Ends the current attribute.

Example

```
$XMLwriterDoc->startAttribute("id");
$XMLwriterDoc->text("1234");
$XMLwriterDoc->endAttribute();

xmlwriter_start_attribute($XMLwriterDoc, "id");
xlmwriter_text($XMLwriterDoc, "1234");
xmlwriter_end_attribute($XMLwriterDoc);
```

endCData()

```
bool XMLWriter::endCData( void )

bool xmlwriter_end_cdata( resource $xmlwriter )
```

Ends the current CDATA section.

Example

```
$XMLwriterDoc->startCData();
$XMLwriterDoc->text("A huge amount of text goes here.");
$XMLwriterDoc->endCData();

xmlwriter_start_cdata($XMLwriterDoc);
xlmwriter_text(
    $XMLwriterDoc, "A huge amount of text goes here."
);
xmlwriter_end_cdata($XMLwriterDoc);
```

endComment()

```
bool XMLWriter::endComment( void )

bool xmlwriter_end_comment( resource $xmlwriter )
```

Ends the current comment.

Example

```
$XMLwriterDoc->startComment();
$XMLwriterDoc->text("Bugs wuz here.");
$XMLwriterDoc->endComment();

xmlwriter_start_comment($XMLwriterDoc);
xlmwriter_text($XMLwriterDoc, "Bugs wuz here.");
xmlwriter_end_comment($XMLwriterDoc);
```

endDocument()

```
bool XMLWriter::endDocument( void )

bool xmlwriter_end_document( resource $xmlwriter )
```

Ends the current document.

Example

```
$XMLwriterDoc->endDocument();

xmlwriter_end_document($XMLwriterDoc);
```

endDTDAttlist()

```
bool XMLWriter::endDTDAttlist( void )

bool xmlwriter_end_dtd_attlist( resource $xmlwriter )
```

Ends the current DTD attribute list.

Tips

XMLWriter's DTD methods are for writing embedded Document type Definitions.

Example

```
$XMLwriterDoc->startDTDAttlist('book');
$XMLwriterDoc->text('id');
$XMLwriterDoc->text(' ID');
$XMLwriterDoc->text(' #REQUIRED');
$XMLwriterDoc->endDTDAttlist();

xmlwriter_start_dtd_attlist($XMLwriterDoc, 'book');
xmlwriter_text($XMLwriterDoc, 'id');
xmlwriter_text($XMLwriterDoc, ' ID');
xmlwriter_text($XMLwriterDoc, ' #REQUIRED');
xmlwriter_end_dtd_attlist($XMLwriterDoc);
```

endDTDElement()

```
bool XMLWriter::endDTDElement( void )

bool xmlwriter_end_dtd_element( resource $xmlwriter )
```

Ends the current DTD element.

Tips

XMLWriter's DTD methods are for writing embedded Document type Definitions.

Example

```
$XMLwriterDoc->startDTDElement('book');
$XMLwriterDoc->text('(#PCDATA)');
$XMLwriterDoc->endDTDElement();

xmlwriter_start_dtd_element($XMLwriterDoc, 'book');
xmlwriter_text($XMLwriterDoc, '(#PCDATA)');
xmlwriter_end_dtd_element($XMLwriterDoc);
```

endDTDEntity()

```
bool XMLWriter::endDTDEntity( void )

bool xmlwriter_end_dtd_entity( resource $xmlwriter )
```

Ends the current DTD entity.

Tips

XMLWriter's DTD methods are for writing embedded Document type Definitions.

Example

```
$XMLwriterDoc->startDTDEntity("copyright", false);
$XMLwriterDoc->text(
    "Copyright (C) 2015, John M. F. Stokes"
);
$XMLwriterDoc->endDTDEntity();

xmlwriter_start_dtd_entity(
    $XMLwriterDoc, "copyright", false
);
xmlwriter_text(
    $XMLwriterDoc, "Copyright (C) 2015, John M. F. Stokes"
);
xmlwriter_end_dtd_entity($XMLwriterDoc);
```

endDTD()

```
bool XMLWriter::endDTD( void )

bool xmlwriter_end_dtd( resource $xmlwriter )
```

Ends the DTD of the document.

Tips

XMLWriter's DTD methods are for writing embedded Document type Definitions.

Example

```
$XMLwriterDoc->startDTD('MyDocType');
//Element and Attribute definitions here
$XMLwriterDoc->endDTD();

xmlwriter_start_dtd($XMLwriterDoc, 'MyDocType');
//Element and Attribute definitions here
xmlwriter_end_dtd($XMLwriterDoc);
```

endElement()

```
bool XMLWriter::endElement( void )

bool xmlwriter_end_element( resource $xmlwriter )
```

Ends the current element.

Tips

Use startElement() and endElement() for elements with attributes or children. For simpler elements, use writeElement().

Example

```
$XMLwriterDoc->startElement('title');
$XMLwriterDoc->text('Firebird: A Trilogy');
$XMLwriterDoc->endElement();

xmlwriter_start_element($XMLwriterDoc, 'title');
xmlwriter_text('Firebird: A Trilogy');
xmlwriter_end_element($XMLwriterDoc);
```

endPI()

```
bool XMLWriter::endPI( void )

bool xmlwriter_end_pi( resource $xmlwriter )
```

Ends the current processing instruction.

Example

```
$XMLwriterDoc->startPI('xml-stylesheet');
$XMLwriterDoc->text('type="text/css"');
$XMLwriterDoc->text(' href="style.css"');
$XMLwriterDoc->endPI();

xmlwriter_start_pi($XMLwriterDoc, 'xml-stylesheet');
xmlwriter_text($XMLwriterDoc, 'type="text/css"');
xmlwriter_text($XMLwriterDoc, ' href="style.css"');
xmlwriter_end_pi($XMLwriterDoc);
```

flush()

```
mixed XMLWriter::flush([ bool $empty = true ] )

mixed xmlwriter_flush( resource $xmlwriter
    [, bool $empty = true ] )
```

Flushes the current buffer.

Tips

If you're building in memory (that is, you started your document with openMemory()),
this has the same effect as calling outputMemory(). Otherwise, it forces a write to disk.

Example

```
$XMLwriterDoc = new XMLWriter();
$XMLwriterDoc->openMemory();
//Build document
echo $XMLwriterDoc->flush();

$XMLwriterDoc = xmlwriter_open_memory();
//Build document
echo xmlwriter_flush($XMLwriterDoc);
```

fullEndElement()

```
bool XMLWriter::fullEndElement( void )

bool xmlwriter_full_end_element( resource $xmlwriter )
```

End the current XML element. Writes an end tag even if the element is empty.

Tips

By default, XMLWriter writes empty elements as self-closed tags, like <book />. To force an opening and closing tag, like <book></book>, use this method instead of endElement().

Example

```
$XMLwriterDoc->startElement('book');
$XMLwriterDoc->endElement(); //Writes <book/>

//Writes <book></book>
$XMLwriterDoc->startElement('book');
$XMLwriterDoc->fullEndElement();

xmlwriter_start_element($XMLwriterDoc, 'book');
xmlwriter_end_element($XMLwriterDoc); //Writes <book/>

//Writes <book></book>
xmlwriter_start_element($XMLwriterDoc, 'book');
xmlwriter_full_end_element($XMLwriterDoc);
```

openMemory()

```
bool XMLWriter::openMemory( void )

resource xmlwriter_open_memory( void )
```

Creates a new XMLWriter using memory for string output.

Example

```
$XMLwriterDoc = new XMLWriter();
$XMLwriterDoc->openMemory();
//Build document
echo $XMLwriterDoc->outputMemory();

$XMLwriterDoc = xmlwriter_open_memory();
//Build document
echo xmlwriter_output_memory($XMLwriterDoc);
```

openURI()

```
bool XMLWriter::openURI( string $uri )

resource xmlwriter_open_uri( string $uri )
```

Creates a new XMLWriter using $uri for the output.

Tips

Use openURI('php://stdout'); to write to screen.

Example

```
$XMLwriterDoc = new XMLWriter();
$XMLwriterDoc->openURI('library.xml');

$XMLwriterDoc = xmlwriter_open_uri('library.xml');
```

outputMemory()

```
string XMLWriter::outputMemory([ bool $flush = true ] )

string xmlwriter_output_memory( resource $xmlwriter
    [, bool $flush = true ] )
```

Returns the current buffer.

Example

```
$XMLwriterDoc = new XMLWriter();
$XMLwriterDoc->openMemory();
//Build document
echo $XMLwriterDoc->outputMemory();

$XMLwriterDoc = xmlwriter_open_memory();
//Build document
echo xmlwriter_output_memory($XMLwriterDoc);
```

setIndentString()

```
bool XMLWriter::setIndentString( string $indentString )

bool xmlwriter_set_indent_string( resource $xmlwriter ,
    string $indentString )
```

Sets the string which will be used to indent each element/attribute of the resulting XML.

Tips

Default indent is two spaces. Remember to also call setIndent().

Example

```
$XMLwriterDoc->setIndent(true);
$XMLwriterDoc->setIndentString("\t");

xmlwriter_set_indent($XMLwriterDoc, true);
xmlwriter_set_indent_string($XMLwriterDoc, "\t");
```

setIndent()

```
bool XMLWriter::setIndent( bool $indent )

bool xmlwriter_set_indent( resource $xmlwriter ,
    bool $indent )
```

Sets indentation on or off.

Example

```
$XMLwriterDoc->setIndent(true);
$XMLwriterDoc->setIndentString("\t");

xmlwriter_set_indent($XMLwriterDoc, true);
xmlwriter_set_indent_string($XMLwriterDoc, "\t");
```

startAttributeNS()

```
bool XMLWriter::startAttributeNS( string $prefix ,
    string $name , string $uri )

bool xmlwriter_start_attribute_ns( resource $xmlwriter ,
    string $prefix , string $name , string $uri )
```

Starts a namespaced attribute.

Tips

Use endAttribute() to close namespaced attributes, just like regular attributes. There isn't a separate end...() call.

Example

```
$XMLwriterDoc->startElement('book');
$XMLwriterDoc->startAttributeNS(
    'mx', 'id', 'library://ns.adobe.com/flex/mx'
);
$XMLwriterDoc->text('1234');
$XMLwriterDoc->endAttribute();

xmlwriter_start_element($XMLwriterDoc, 'book');
xmlwriter_start_attribute_ns(
    $XMLwriterDoc,
    'mx',
    'id',
    'library://ns.adobe.com/flex/mx'
);
xlmwriter_text($XMLwriterDoc, '1234');
xmlwriter_end_attribute($XMLwriterDoc);
```

startAttribute()

```
bool XMLWriter::startAttribute( string $name )

bool xmlwriter_start_attribute( resource $xmlwriter ,
    string $name )
```

Starts an attribute.

Example

```
$XMLwriterDoc->startElement('book');
$XMLwriterDoc->startAttribute('id');
$XMLwriterDoc->text('1234');
$XMLwriterDoc->endAttribute();

xmlwriter_start_element($XMLwriterDoc, 'book');
xmlwriter_start_attribute($XMLwriterDoc, 'id');
xlmwriter_text($XMLwriterDoc, '1234');
xmlwriter_end_attribute($XMLwriterDoc);
```

startCData()

```
bool XMLWriter::startCData( void )

bool xmlwriter_start_cdata( resource $xmlwriter )
```

Starts a CDATA block.

Example

```
$XMLwriterDoc->startCData();
$XMLwriterDoc->text("A huge amount of text goes here.");
$XMLwriterDoc->endCData();

xmlwriter_start_cdata($XMLwriterDoc);
xlmwriter_text(
    $XMLwriterDoc, "A huge amount of text goes here."
);
xmlwriter_end_cdata($XMLwriterDoc);
```

startComment()

```
bool XMLWriter::startComment( void )

bool xmlwriter_start_comment( resource $xmlwriter )
```

Starts a comment.

Example

```
$XMLwriterDoc->startComment();
$XMLwriterDoc->text("Bugs wuz here.");
$XMLwriterDoc->endComment();

xmlwriter_start_comment($XMLwriterDoc);
xlmwriter_text($XMLwriterDoc, "Bugs wuz here.");
xmlwriter_end_comment($XMLwriterDoc);
```

startDocument()

```
bool XMLWriter::startDocument([ string $version = 1.0
    [, string $encoding = NULL [, string $standalone ]]] )

bool xmlwriter_start_document( resource $xmlwriter
    [, string $version = 1.0 [, string $encoding = NULL
    [, string $standalone ]]] )
```

Starts a document.

Example

```
$XMLwriterDoc = new XMLWriter();
$XMLwriterDoc->openURI('library.xml');
$XMLwriterDoc->startDocument('1.0','utf-8');
//Build document
$XMLwriterDoc->endDocument();

$XMLwriterDoc = xmlwriter_open_uri('library.xml');
xmlwriter_start_document($XMLwriterDoc, '1.0','utf-8');
//Build document
xmlwriter_end_document($XMLwriterDoc);
```

startDTDAttlist()

```
bool XMLWriter::startDTDAttlist( string $name )

bool xmlwriter_start_dtd_attlist( resource $xmlwriter ,
    string $name )
```

Starts a DTD attribute list.

Tips

XMLWriter's DTD methods are for writing embedded Document type Definitions.

Example

```
$XMLwriterDoc->startDTDAttlist('book');
$XMLwriterDoc->text('id');
$XMLwriterDoc->text(' ID');
$XMLwriterDoc->text(' #REQUIRED');
$XMLwriterDoc->endDTDAttlist();

xmlwriter_start_dtd_attlist($XMLwriterDoc, 'book');
xmlwriter_text($XMLwriterDoc, 'id');
xmlwriter_text($XMLwriterDoc, ' ID');
xmlwriter_text($XMLwriterDoc, ' #REQUIRED');
xmlwriter_end_dtd_attlist($XMLwriterDoc);
```

startDTDElement()

```
bool XMLWriter::startDTDElement( string $qualifiedName )

bool xmlwriter_start_dtd_element( resource $xmlwriter ,
    string $qualifiedName ))
```

Starts a DTD element.

Tips

XMLWriter's DTD methods are for writing embedded Document type Definitions.

Example

```
$XMLwriterDoc->startDTDElement('book');
$XMLwriterDoc->text('(#PCDATA)');
$XMLwriterDoc->endDTDElement();

xmlwriter_start_dtd_element($XMLwriterDoc, 'book');
xmlwriter_text($XMLwriterDoc, '(#PCDATA)');
xmlwriter_end_dtd_element($XMLwriterDoc);
```

startDTDEntity()

```
bool XMLWriter::startDTDEntity( string $name ,
    bool $isparam )

bool xmlwriter_start_dtd_entity( resource $xmlwriter ,
    string $name , bool $isparam )
```

Starts a DTD entity.

Tips

The $isparam boolean indicates whether you're creating a Parameter Entity (true) or a General Entity (false). Note that it has no default, so you'll have to pass a boolean. In most cases, use false.

Example

```
$XMLwriterDoc->startDTDEntity("copyright", false);
$XMLwriterDoc->text(
    "Copyright (C) 2015, John M. F. Stokes"
);
$XMLwriterDoc->endDTDEntity();

xmlwriter_start_dtd_entity(
    $XMLwriterDoc, "copyright", false
);
xmlwriter_text(
    $XMLwriterDoc, "Copyright (C) 2015, John M. F. Stokes"
);
xmlwriter_end_dtd_entity($XMLwriterDoc);
```

startDTD( )

```
bool XMLWriter::startDTD( string $qualifiedName
    [, string $publicId [, string $systemId ]] )

bool xmlwriter_start_dtd( resource $xmlwriter ,
    string $qualifiedName [, string $publicId
    [, string $systemId ]] )
```

Starts a Document Type Definition.

Tips

XMLWriter's DTD methods are for writing embedded Document type Definitions.

Example

```
$XMLwriterDoc->startDTD('MyDocType');
//Element and Attribute definitions here
$XMLwriterDoc->endDTD();

xmlwriter_start_dtd($XMLwriterDoc, 'MyDocType');
//Element and Attribute definitions here
xmlwriter_end_dtd($XMLwriterDoc);
```

startElementNS( )

```
bool XMLWriter::startElementNS( string $prefix ,
    string $name , string $uri )

bool xmlwriter_start_element_ns( resource $xmlwriter ,
    string $prefix , string $name , string $uri )
```

Starts a namespaced element.

Tips

Use startElement( ) and endElement( ) for elements with attributes or children. For simpler elements, use writeElement( ).

Example

```
$XMLwriterDoc->startElementNS('mx', 'series',
    'library://ns.adobe.com/flex/mx' );
$XMLwriterDoc->text('25,32,46' );
$XMLwriterDoc->endElement( );

xmlwriter_start_elementNS($XMLwriterDoc, 'mx',
    'series', 'library://ns.adobe.com/flex/mx' );
xmlwriter_text($XMLwriterDoc, '25,32,46' );
xmlwriter_end_element($XMLwriterDoc);
```

startElement( )

```
bool XMLWriter::startElement( string $name )

bool xmlwriter_start_element( resource $xmlwriter ,
    string $name )
```

Create start element tag

Tips

Use startElement( ) and endElement( ) for elements with attributes or children. For simpler elements, use writeElement( ).

Example

```
$XMLwriterDoc->startElement('title' );
$XMLwriterDoc->text('Firebird: A Trilogy' );
$XMLwriterDoc->endElement( );

xmlwriter_start_element($XMLwriterDoc, 'title' );
xmlwriter_text('Firebird: A Trilogy' );
xmlwriter_end_element($XMLwriterDoc);
```

startPI()

```
bool XMLWriter::startPI( string $target )

bool xmlwriter_start_pi( resource $xmlwriter ,
    string $target )
```

Starts a processing instruction tag.

Tips

Attributes to a Processing instruction must be added with text(), not writeAttribute().

Example

```
$XMLwriterDoc->startPI('xml-stylesheet');
$XMLwriterDoc->text('type="text/css"');
$XMLwriterDoc->text(' href="style.css"');
$XMLwriterDoc->endPI();

xmlwriter_start_pi($XMLwriterDoc, 'xml-stylesheet');
xmlwriter_text($XMLwriterDoc, 'type="text/css"');
xmlwriter_text($XMLwriterDoc, ' href="style.css"');
xmlwriter_end_pi($XMLwriterDoc);
```

text()

```
bool XMLWriter::text( string $content )

bool xmlwriter_text( resource $xmlwriter , string $content )
```

Writes a text node.

Tips

Calling text() with an empty string will force XMLWriter to write a closing > on a tag opened with startElement().

Example

```
$XMLwriterDoc->startElement('title');
$XMLwriterDoc->text('Firebird: A Trilogy');
$XMLwriterDoc->endElement();

xmlwriter_start_element($XMLwriterDoc, 'title');
xmlwriter_text('Firebird: A Trilogy');
xmlwriter_end_element($XMLwriterDoc);
```

writeAttributeNS()

```
bool XMLWriter::writeAttributeNS( string $prefix ,
    string $name , string $uri , string $content )

bool xmlwriter_write_attribute_ns( resource $xmlwriter ,
    string $prefix , string $name , string $uri ,
    string $content )
```

Writes a full namespaced attribute.

Example

```
$XMLwriterDoc->startElement('book');
$XMLwriterDoc->writeAttributeNS(
    'mx', 'id', 'library://ns.adobe.com/flex/mx', '1234'
);
$XMLwriterDoc->endAttribute();

xmlwriter_start_element($XMLwriterDoc, 'book');
xmlwriter_write_attribute_ns(
    $XMLwriterDoc, 'mx', 'id',
    'library://ns.adobe.com/flex/mx', '1234'
);
xmlwriter_end_attribute($XMLwriterDoc);
```

writeAttribute()

```
bool XMLWriter::writeAttribute( string $name , string $value )

bool xmlwriter_write_attribute( resource $xmlwriter ,
    string $name , string $value )
```

Writes a full attribute.

Example

```
$XMLwriterDoc->startElement('book');
$XMLwriterDoc->writeAttribute('ISBN','978-0764229275');

xmlwriter_start_element($XMLwriterDoc,'book');
xmlwriter_write_attribute(
    $XMLwriterDoc, 'ISBN', '978-0764229275'
);
```

writeCData()

```
bool XMLWriter::writeCData( string $content )

bool xmlwriter_write_cdata( resource $xmlwriter ,
    string $content )
```

Writes a full CDATA block.

Example

```
$XMLwriterDoc->writeCData('Lots of text here...');

xmlwriter_write_cdata($XMLwriterDoc,'Lots of text here...');
```

writeComment()

```
bool XMLWriter::writeComment( string $content )

bool xmlwriter_write_comment( resource $xmlwriter ,
    string $content ))
```

Write full comment tag.

Example

```
$XMLwriterDoc->writeComment('Bugs wuz here.');

xmlwriter_write_comment($XMLwriterDoc,'Bugs wuz here.');
```

writeDTDAttlist()

```
bool XMLWriter::writeDTDAttlist( string $name , string $content )

bool xmlwriter_write_dtd_attlist( resource $xmlwriter ,
    string $name , string $content )
```

Writes a DTD attribute list.

Example

```
$XMLwriterDoc->writeDTDAttlist('book', 'id ID #REQUIRED');

xmlwriter_write_dtd_attlist(
    $XMLwriterDoc, 'book', 'id ID #REQUIRED'
);
```

writeDTDElement()

```
bool XMLWriter::writeDTDElement( string $name , string $content )

bool xmlwriter_write_dtd_element( resource $xmlwriter ,
    string $name , string $content )
```

Write full DTD element tag.

Example

```
$XMLwriterDoc->writeDTDElement('book', '(#PCDATA)');

xmlwriter_write_dtd_element(
    $XMLwriterDoc, 'book', '(#PCDATA)'
);
```

writeDTDEntity()

```
bool XMLWriter::writeDTDEntity( string $name ,
    string $content , bool $pe , string $pubid ,
    string $sysid , string $ndataid )

bool xmlwriter_write_dtd_entity( resource $xmlwriter ,
    string $name , string $content , bool $pe ,
    string $pubid , string $sysid , string $ndataid )
```

Write full DTD Entity tag.

Tips

$entitye is a boolean indicating whether this is a parameter entity (true) or a general entity (false).

Example

```
$XMLwriterDoc->writeDTDEntity(
    'copyright', 'Copyright (C) 2015,
    John M. F. Stokes', false
);

xmlwriter_write_dtd_entity(
    $XMLwriterDoc,
    'copyright', 'Copyright (C) 2015,
    John M. F. Stokes', false
);
```

writeDTD()

```
bool XMLWriter::writeDTD( string $name
    [, string $publicId [, string $systemId
    [, string $subset ]]] )

bool xmlwriter_write_dtd( resource $xmlwriter ,
    string $name [, string $publicId [, string $systemId
    [, string $subset ]]] )
```

Write full DTD tag.

Tips

This will generally be used for external DTDs, like XHTML.

Example

```
$XMLwriterDoc->writeDTD(
    'html', '-//W3C//DTD XHTML 1.0 Strict//EN',
    'http://www.w3.org/TR/xhtml1/DTD/xhtml1-strict.dtd'
);

xmlwriter_write_dtd(
    $XMLwriterDoc,
    'html', '-//W3C//DTD XHTML 1.0 Strict//EN',
    'http://www.w3.org/TR/xhtml1/DTD/xhtml1-strict.dtd'
);
```

writeElementNS()

```
bool XMLWriter::writeElementNS( string $prefix ,
    string $name , string $uri [, string $content ] )

bool xmlwriter_write_element_ns( resource $xmlwriter ,
    string $prefix , string $name , string $uri
    [, string $content ] ))
```

Writes a full namespaced element tag.

Example

```
$XMLwriterDoc->writeElementNS(
    'mx', 'series', library://ns.adobe.com/flex/mx',
    '25,32,46'
);

xmlwriter_write_element_ns(
    $XMLwriterDoc,
    'mx', 'series', 'library://ns.adobe.com/flex/mx',
    '25,32,46'
);
```

writeElement()

```
bool XMLWriter::writeElement( string $name
    [, string $content ] )

bool xmlwriter_write_element( resource $xmlwriter ,
    string $name [, string $content ] )
```

Writes a full element tag.

Example

```
$XMLwriterDoc->writeElement('title','Firebird: A Trilogy');

xmlwriter_write_element(
    $XMLwriterDoc, 'title', 'Firebird: A Trilogy'
);
```

writePI()

```
bool XMLWriter::writePI( string $target , string $content )

bool xmlwriter_write_pi( resource $xmlwriter ,
    string $target , string $content )
```

Writes a processing instruction.

Example

```
$XMLwriterDoc->writePI(
    'xml-stylesheet', 'type="text/css" href="style.css"'
);

xmlwriter_write_pi(
    $XMLwriterDoc,
    'xml-stylesheet', 'type="text/css" href="style.css"'
);
```

writeRaw()

```
bool XMLWriter::writeRaw( string $content )

bool xmlwriter_write_raw( resource $xmlwriter ,
    string $content )
```

Writes a raw XML text node.

Tips

Use this to write blocks of preexisting XML text to your output document. This is the closest XMLWriter comes to modifying an existing document.

Example

```
$XMLwriterDoc->startElement('book');
$XMLwriterDoc->writeRaw(
    '<title>Firebird: A Trilogy</title>'
);
$XMLwriterDoc->endElement();

xmlwriter_start_element($XMLwriterDoc,'book');
xmlwriter_write_raw(
    $XMLwriterDoc,
    '<title>Firebird: A Trilogy</title>'
);
xmlwriter_end_element($XMLwriterDoc);
```

Appendix
D

library.xml

Listing D: library.xml

```xml
<?xml version="1.0" encoding="utf-8"?>
<library>
    <book id="B1" ISBN="NA">
        <title>Pride and Prejudice</title>
        <author>Jane Austen</author>
        <pages>416</pages>
        <format>Hardback</format>
        <publisher>T. Egerton, Whitehall</publisher>
        <year>1813</year>
        <language>English</language>
    </book>
    <book id="B2" ISBN="NA">
        <title>The Adventures of Sherlock Holmes</title>
        <author>Arthur Conan Doyle</author>
        <pages>307</pages>
        <format>Hardback</format>
        <publisher>George Newnes</publisher>
```

```xml
        <year>1892</year>
        <language>English</language>
        <excerpt>
            <![CDATA[
    Sherlock Holmes\'s quick eye took in my occupation, and
he shook his head with a smile as he noticed my questioning
glances. "Beyond the obvious facts that he has at some time
done manual labor, that he takes snuff, that he is a
Freemason, that he has been in China, and that he has done a
considerable amount of writing lately, I can deduce nothing else."
            ]]>
        </excerpt>
    </book>
    <book id="B3" ISBN="NA">
        <title>Alice's Adventures in Wonderland</title>
        <author>Lewis Carroll</author>
        <pages>202</pages>
        <format>Hardback</format>
        <publisher>Macmillan</publisher>
        <year>1865</year>
        <language>English</language>
    </book>
    <book id="B4" ISBN="NA">
        <title>A Christmas Carol</title>
        <author>Charles Dickens</author>
        <pages>128</pages>
        <format>Hardback</format>
        <publisher>Chapman and Hall</publisher>
        <year>1843</year>
        <language>English</language>
    </book>
    <book id="B5" ISBN="0765328321">
        <title>Halo: The Fall of Reach</title>
        <author>Eric Nylund</author>
        <pages>448</pages>
        <format>Paperback</format>
        <publisher>Tor</publisher>
        <year>2010</year>
        <language>English</language>
    </book>
</library>
```

Appendix E

FlexDoc.xml

Adapted from the Apache Flex project's online documentation at
https://flex.apache.org/asdoc/mx/charts/LineChart.html.

Listing E: FlexDoc.xml

```
<?xml version="1.0"?>
<!--

  Licensed to the Apache Software Foundation (ASF) under one
or more contributor license agreements.  See the NOTICE file
distributed with this work for additional information regarding
copyright ownership. The ASF licenses this file to You under the
Apache License, Version 2.0 (the "License"); you may not use this
file except in compliance with the License.  You may obtain a copy
of the License at

    http://www.apache.org/licenses/LICENSE-2.0
```

Unless required by applicable law or agreed to in writing, software distributed under the License is distributed on an "AS IS" BASIS, WITHOUT WARRANTIES OR CONDITIONS OF ANY KIND, either express or implied. See the License for the specific language governing permissions and limitations under the License.

```
-->
<!-- Simple example to demonstrate the LineChart and AreaChart
controls. -->
<s:Application xmlns:fx="http://ns.adobe.com/mxml/2009"
    xmlns:s="library://ns.adobe.com/flex/spark"
    xmlns:mx="library://ns.adobe.com/flex/mx">

    <fx:Script>
        <![CDATA[

        import mx.collections.ArrayCollection;

        [Bindable]
        private var expensesAC:ArrayCollection =
            new ArrayCollection( [
                { Month: "Jan", Profit: 2000,
                  Expenses: 1500, Amount: 450 },
                { Month: "Feb", Profit: 1000,
                  Expenses: 200, Amount: 600 },
                { Month: "Mar", Profit: 1500,
                  Expenses: 500, Amount: 300 },
                { Month: "Apr", Profit: 1800,
                  Expenses: 1200, Amount: 900 },
                { Month: "May", Profit: 2400,
                  Expenses: 575, Amount: 500 }
            ]);
        ]]>
    </fx:Script>

    <fx:Declarations>
        <!-- Define custom colors for use as fills in the
AreaChart control. -->
        <mx:SolidColor id="sc1" color="blue" alpha=".3"/>
        <mx:SolidColor id="sc2" color="red" alpha=".3"/>
        <mx:SolidColor id="sc3" color="green" alpha=".3"/>

        <!-- Define custom Strokes. -->
        <mx:SolidColorStroke id = "s1"
            color="blue" weight="2"/>
        <mx:SolidColorStroke id = "s2"
            color="red" weight="2"/>
```

```
    <mx:SolidColorStroke id = "s3"
        color="green" weight="2"/>
</fx:Declarations>

<mx:Panel
    title="LineChart and AreaChart Controls Example"
    height="100%" width="100%" layout="horizontal">

    <mx:LineChart id="linechart"
        height="100%" width="45%"
        paddingLeft="5" paddingRight="5"
        showDataTips="true" dataProvider="{expensesAC}">

        <mx:horizontalAxis>
            <mx:CategoryAxis categoryField="Month"/>
        </mx:horizontalAxis>

        <mx:series>
            <mx:LineSeries yField="Profit" form="curve"
                displayName="Profit"
                lineStroke="{s1}"/>
            <mx:LineSeries yField="Expenses" form="curve"
                displayName="Expenses"
                lineStroke="{s2}"/>
            <mx:LineSeries yField="Amount" form="curve"
                displayName="Amount"
                lineStroke="{s3}"/>
        </mx:series>
    </mx:LineChart>

    <mx:Legend dataProvider="{linechart}"/>

    <mx:AreaChart id="Areachart"
        height="100%" width="45%"
        paddingLeft="5" paddingRight="5"
        showDataTips="true" dataProvider="{expensesAC}">

        <mx:horizontalAxis>
            <mx:CategoryAxis categoryField="Month"/>
        </mx:horizontalAxis>

        <mx:series>
            <mx:AreaSeries yField="Profit"
                form="curve" displayName="Profit"
                areaStroke="{s1}" areaFill="{sc1}"/>
```

```
            <mx:AreaSeries yField="Expenses"
                form="curve" displayName="Expenses"
                areaStroke="{s2}" areaFill="{sc2}"/>
            <mx:AreaSeries yField="Amount"
                form="curve" displayName="Amount"
                areaStroke="{s3}" areaFill="{sc3}"/>
        </mx:series>
    </mx:AreaChart>

    <mx:Legend dataProvider="{Areachart}"/>

    </mx:Panel>
</s:Application>
```

Appendix F

Libxml Constants

CONSTANT	Description
LIBXML_COMPACT	Activate small nodes allocation optimization. This may speed up your application without needing to change the code. *Only available in Libxml >= 2.6.21*
LIBXML_DTDATTR	Default DTD attributes
LIBXML_DTDLOAD	Load the external subset
LIBXML_DTDVALID	Validate with the DTD
LIBXML_HTML_NOIMPLIED	Sets HTML_PARSE_NOIMPLIED flag, which turns off the automatic adding of implied html/body... elements. *Only available in Libxml >= 2.7.7 (as of PHP >= 5.4.0)*
LIBXML_HTML_NODEFDTD	Sets HTML_PARSE_NODEFDTD flag, which prevents a default doctype being added when one is not found. *Only available in Libxml >= 2.7.8 (as of PHP >= 5.4.0)*
LIBXML_NOBLANKS	Remove blank nodes

CONSTANT	Description
LIBXML_NOCDATA	Merge CDATA as text nodes
LIBXML_NOEMPTYTAG	Expand empty tags (e.g. ` ` to ` </br>`). *This option is currently just available in the* `DOMDocument::save` *and* `DOMDocument::saveXML` *functions.*
LIBXML_NOENT	Substitute entities
LIBXML_NOERROR	Suppress error reports
LIBXML_NONET	Disable network access when loading documents
LIBXML_NOWARNING	Suppress warning reports
LIBXML_NOXMLDECL	Drop the XML declaration when saving a document. *Only available in Libxml >= 2.6.21*
LIBXML_NSCLEAN	Remove redundant namespace declarations
LIBXML_PARSEHUGE	Sets `XML_PARSE_HUGE` flag, which relaxes any hardcoded limit from the parser. This affects limits like maximum depth of a document or the entity recursion, as well as limits of the size of text nodes. *Available in Libxml >= 2.7.0 (as of PHP >= 5.3.2 and PHP >= 5.2.12)*
LIBXML_PEDANTIC	Sets `XML_PARSE_PEDANTIC` flag, which enables pedantic error reporting. *Available as of PHP >= 5.4.0*
LIBXML_XINCLUDE	Implement XInclude substitution
LIBXML_ERR_ERROR	A recoverable error
LIBXML_ERR_FATAL	A fatal error
LIBXML_ERR_NONE	No errors
LIBXML_ERR_WARNING	A simple warning
LIBXML_VERSION	libxml version like 20605 or 20617
LIBXML_DOTTED_VERSION	libxml version like 2.6.5 or 2.6.17
LIBXML_SCHEMA_CREATE	Create default/fixed value nodes during XSD schema validation. *Available in Libxml >= 2.6.14 (as of PHP >= 5.5.2)*

Printed in Great Britain
by Amazon

33553528R00128